THE
ART AND POLITICS
OF ACADEMIC
GOVERNANCE

THE ART
AND POLITICS
OF ACADEMIC
GOVERNANCE

*Relations among Boards,
Presidents, and Faculty*

Kenneth P. Mortimer
and Colleen O'Brien Sathre

AMERICAN COUNCIL ON EDUCATION
PRAEGER
Series on Higher Education

Library of Congress Cataloging-in-Publication Data

Mortimer, Kenneth P., 1937–
   The art and politics of academic governance : relations among boards,
presidents, and faculty / Kenneth P. Mortimer and Colleen O'Brien
Sathre.
      p. cm. — (ACE/Praeger series on higher education)
   Includes bibliographical references and index.
   ISBN-13: 978–0–275–98478–6
   ISBN-10: 0–275–98478–8
   1. Universities and colleges—United States—Administration.
2. Education, Higher—United States—Administration.   I. Sathre,
Colleen O'Brien .   II. Title.
   LB2341.M6397   2007
   378.1'01 2 22   2007000496

British Library Cataloguing in Publication Data is available.

Library of Congress Catalog Card Number: 2007000496
ISBN-13: 978–0–275–98478–6
ISBN-10: 0–275–98478–8

First published in 2007

Praeger Publishers, 88 Post Road West, Westport, CT 06881
An imprint of Greenwood Publishing Group, Inc.
www.praeger.com

Printed in the United States of America

The paper used in this book complies with the
Permanent Paper Standard issued by the National
Information Standards Organization (Z39.48–1984).

10 9 8 7 6 5 4 3 2 1

January 9, 2008

In loving memory of Lorrie Mortimer

CONTENTS

PREFACE

This book is based on research, commentary, and the literature on governance. More important, it reflects our combined experience as researchers, vice presidents, consultants, and as a president of two public institutions. Using case studies based on actual events, we illustrate the challenges faced in the practice of shared governance when institutions confront big issues such as program closure, institutional planning and resource allocation, multicampus relationships, and tuition setting.

This book focuses on the relationships among boards, administrators, and faculty as governance partners and does not seek to elevate the role of any one party. It is concerned with what happens in the messy world of governance on the controversial issues. It uses concepts such as issue salience, timing, and positioning to help make the case that treatments of governance are often inadequate because they fail to consider the role of politics in decision and implementation processes. In this regard, this book is political in tone; it stresses that differences in power, authority, and influence are basic realities and a legitimate part of the *art* of governance.

We would like to acknowledge Jerry Gaff and his colleague Bridget Puzon, who have kindly given us permission to cite and quote from their unpublished work, "What if the Faculty *Really Do* Assume Responsibility for the Instructional Program?" References to this paper are found in Chapter 4 and have enriched our discussion of programs and curriculum. We thank and acknowledge Neil Hamilton for adding to our defense of healthy shared governance in Chapter 7 by giving us permission to reference and quote from his white paper, "The Future of Shared Governance." Our initial work on the role of politics in the art of governance, including a discussion of external forces, the school closure case, and relations among boards, faculty, and administrators (Mortimer and Sathre 2006), appeared in *Governance and the Public Good*, edited by William G. Tierney and published by SUNY Press, © 2006. These topics have been expanded and appear with permission in Chapters 1, 2, and 3 of this book. Finally, we are indebted to Frank Newman for the many insights into governance that he shared over the years. His wisdom has influenced this book, and Frank's death saddens us all.

We acknowledge the American Council on Education staff, especially Wendy Bresler, and Susan Slesinger at Greenwood Publishing for encouraging and supporting our work on this book. When we encountered delays, their patience and support were a great relief.

A book of this sort could only come about as a result of years of experience with governing board members, fellow administrators, and faculty colleagues. For all of the times they supported our efforts, challenged us to be better leaders, and yes, pointed out the errors of our ways, we say thanks. And to Jean Imada and Masayo Matsukawa, who always made our workdays and lives better, you are the best! One always has the feeling that if one were to do it over, one might get more of it right the next time. But never fear, retirement is too good to think such thoughts. Our thanks to Linda K. Johnsrud and Dennis P. Jones for reading and offering comments on drafts of this book, and to the Friday night gang (you know who you are) for your encouragement and insights on university governance—a topic we never tire of discussing. Finally, this book would not have happened without Eugene Sathre's precise and ever-cheerful editorial assistance.

Kenneth P. Mortimer
Colleen O'Brien Sathre

ABBREVIATIONS

AA	Associate of Arts
AAC&U	Association of American Colleges and Universities
AAUP	American Association of University Professors
ACE	American Council on Education
AFT	American Federation of Teachers
AGB	Association of Governing Boards of Universities and Colleges
CAO	Chief Academic Officer
CHEPA	Center for Higher Education Policy Analysis
CPEC	California Postsecondary Education Commission
CPO	Chief Planning Officer
ECS	Education Commission of the States

MSU   Mythical State University

NCHEMS   National Center for Higher Education Management
             Systems

NLRA   National Labor Relations Act

NLRB   National Labor Relations Board

State U   State University

USDOE   United States Department of Education

VPAA   Vice President for Academic Affairs

INTRODUCTION

A s astute observers of decision making in government, business, or higher education realize, governance is an art form. It involves the capacity to deal with staggering levels of complexity—competing interests and agendas, an extraordinary range of participants/actors, and negotiations and trade-offs that lead to progress and very often setbacks. Effective governance requires attention to time constraints, personalities, and the importance of collegiality and bureaucracy in the decision-making process. Governing a university surely is not the same as governing the country, but politically savvy behavior is needed in higher education far more than most would like to admit. Politically savvy leaders operate within an environment that gives great deference to process, but are aware and responsive to the larger community's impatience with this legendary characteristic of the academy.

Market and related external forces are holding higher education accountable for results rather than process. These results can include demands for graduates who think critically and solve problems, fill specific workforce needs, work collaboratively, get the job done, show up on time, and pass a drug test. Institutions are becoming more entrepreneurial as they are challenged to develop new revenue streams and demonstrate results for significant societal investments in science and technology—the commercial success of spin-offs. Colleges and universities are competing with other segments of society for public and private resources and go to considerable lengths to demonstrate their accountability in the form of institutional benchmark and performance measures, including graduation rates, the earning power of graduates, and affordable tuition rates. The market is clearly far more interested in results than it is in higher education's internal governance processes. The market does not dictate governance processes, and in this matter higher education institutions are on their own.

What does this mean for the shared governance model, the gold standard for how best to govern higher education? This book revisits the tenets and legitimacy inherent in shared governance. Basically, we argue that shared governance structures work well for the routine business of the academy, but are less effective when the "big issues" are on the table. In focusing on big issues, we draw on earlier treatments of governance processes when faced with "hard decisions" (Eckel 2000) or "big decisions" (Keller 1983; Schuster et al. 1994). On the big issues—whether they involve academic policy, finances, personnel, or strategic directions—academic leaders, whether they are trustees, administrators, or faculty, must recognize and be prepared to function within a process that is likely to be dominated by the political model and the rules of advocacy. Each partner in the decision-making process will defend his or her special interests. Conflicts and arguments in favor of, or opposed to, these interests will be very public, decisions will be reviewed and revisited many times, and the welfare of the whole will take second place or even slip from view.

The art of shared governance requires a partnership of leaders who are *market-smart*—able to understand the market and other external forces at work; *mission-centered*—able to keep their institution's basic goals and distinctive purposes at the forefront of the decision-making process; and *politically savvy*—able to lead their institution safely through the jungle of competing advocates. Leaders and governance participants need to recognize the importance of *all* of these attributes, but different ones can dominate depending on the nature of the big issue at hand. Mastering the skills associated with these attributes will not guarantee results pleasing to all parties, but will go a long way toward building the trust and legitimacy so necessary for effective academic governance.

In Chapter 1 the dilemmas facing a university president and the unexpected consequences of a tuition decision illustrate a real world context for considering the external forces that impact how shared governance unfolds in the modern university setting.

Chapter 2 describes the dynamics of power and influence within higher education and the role of senates and unions. This discussion contributes to a better understanding of how disputes and time-consuming debates about process—procedural correctness—arise in a shared governance environment.

In Chapter 3 we recognize the differences in perceptions of legitimate behavior that are particularly common in relationships between trustees and faculty and the need to ameliorate them if the art of governance is to be effective. The case of closing a school at a public research university is used to illustrate the interactions of boards, administrators, and faculty on a significant issue.

Chapter 4 explores the nature of academic program evolution and discusses the conflict that can emerge when a program of study is viewed as both a faculty and a corporate responsibility. The associate degree transfer case in a multicampus system of two- and four-year institutions is used to illustrate the governance issues that arise when there are legitimate and disputed claims about who, when, and how such matters should be decided.

The basic premise of Chapter 5 is that the president-provost (chief academic officer) partnership is not well understood and that the dynamics of the relationship are crucial to the political nature of governance in higher education. Several cases illustrate how difficult it is in practice to develop a president-provost team and how this shortfall can limit executive leadership and lead to difficulties when establishing priorities for the big issues.

Chapter 6 focuses on strategic planning as a big issue in governance. A synopsis of four strategic planning processes at a higher education system is used to provide the context for an analysis of participation claims, decision making, and lessons learned.

We close in Chapter 7 with a defense of shared governance. We offer observations and suggestions about how the academy can share authority in ways that both reinforce claims for legitimate participation and further institutional responsiveness to market forces and the big issues.

CHAPTER

The World Is Changing Faster Than
the Governance Structure

Institutions ignore a changing environment at their peril. Like dinosaurs, they risk becoming exhibits in a kind of cultural Jurassic Park: places of great interest and curiosity, increasingly irrelevant in a world that has passed them by. Higher education cannot afford to let this happen.
—Kellogg Commission, *Taking Charge of Change*

"Be mission-sensitive and market-smart." These were the words President Jones was mulling over on a Sunday evening, the only time left on a crowded university president's schedule. The week was dominated by conflicting and even confusing demands to be a better advocate for faculty interests, develop a more responsive institution to better serve a diverse set of state needs, and streamline the university and stop trying to be all things to all people. These urgings of the faculty, legislature, community members, and the board seemed to be irreconcilable. How could one possibly be an advocate, be more responsive, and streamline the university at the same time? And the president was worried about the volatility of state appropriations. For some time, funding per student had been declining while tuition was rising precipitously. In this maze of conflicting pressures and interests, who was speaking for the students?

Given the current context of the institution, President Jones sensed that the traditional internal governance processes of the university were not adequately dealing with these competing demands. The impact of universal postsecondary education, rising market forces, increased calls for entrepreneurship, and the need to adopt mission-centered, market-smart strategies constituted a confusing environment for the traditional shared governance processes of the university. The president believed that changing or adapting governance processes to these new realities was one of the major challenges to be faced in leading an institution at the beginning of the twenty-first century.

The reflections of President Jones capture a central thesis of this book, namely, that changes in the external environment of colleges and universities require that internal governance adapt and become more responsive. The case will be made that, in addition to being mission-centered while being market-smart, shared governance partners must also be *politically savvy*. In their recent book, Zemsky, Wegner, and Massy (2005, 13–14) counsel higher education institutions to learn "how to be market-smart to remain mission-centered" and to understand that doing so "means being politically savvy." These scholars provide a rich treatment of the importance of politically savvy perspectives when dealing with market forces in order to craft a higher education agenda for the public good. By contrast, the focus of our book is on the internal governance of universities and colleges and the value of politically savvy behavior on the part of the academy's shared governance partners—boards, administrators, and faculty.

For those institutions where everything is (as the Irish would say) *grand*, a more useful read may be found elsewhere. For faculty and administrative leaders of institutions that identify in part or whole with the dilemmas facing President Jones, it is suggested that being politically savvy is an art form that deserves more attention than is usual in the practice of academic governance.

In this chapter, the events that surrounded the initial rejection and subsequent approval of tuition increases by a governing board are used to illustrate the inter-actions of governing boards, administrators, faculty, and students when external events overtake an otherwise routine bureaucratic task. The intent is to bring an all-important institutional context to the governance discussion. We recognize that this case illustrates only a particular external event that complicated internal governance. Therefore, following the discussion of case dynamics, we expand on an earlier treatment of external influences (Mortimer and Sathre 2006, 80–83) and draw on selections from the literature for a sampling of external forces that are impacting shared governance at institutions in general. How to adapt and enhance shared governance in light of these external forces is a major challenge for the modern higher education institution.

THE TUITION CASE

Decisions

At a spring meeting, a proposed five-year tuition schedule was rejected by the governing board of a statewide system of higher education (referred to here as the University). The next spring, this board approved a five-year tuition schedule that was nearly identical to the one rejected a year earlier.

Background

During the 1970s and 1980s, tuition increases at the University were sporadic. Throughout this period tuition revenues were deposited to the state general fund and were not a factor in determining the University's state support. Beginning in the mid 1980s, and reflecting indirectly the general fund support provided, the governing board approved gradual, modest tuition increases.

As the state's financial outlook dimmed in the early 1990s, state political leaders were not willing to subsidize the University at the levels of the past and asked why the institution didn't increase tuition more, perhaps even double it. As an incentive, legislation was introduced that would return to the University *some* tuition revenue; it did not pass and annual modest tuition increases continued.

The state's financial condition continued to worsen, and by the mid 1990s the legislature acted to fundamentally change the financing structure of the University. All tuition revenues were returned to the institution. General funds were reduced by a similar amount, however, and on such short notice that the administration and board were forced to make up at least part of the budget short-fall by means of a 50 percent tuition increase for one year, followed by a 20-plus percent increase the next year.

The president had testified against returning tuition revenues to the University, arguing that unless there were assurances that future tuition revenues would not be treated as offsets against the general fund appropriation, there was every likelihood that the result would be higher tuition and no improvement in services. The final legislative committee considering the matter added a base budget commitment to the bill and it passed. The state's dire economic condition continued in subsequent years, however, and the state never honored its base budget commitment. Eventually this commitment was removed from state law and the president's worst fears were realized.

The economic condition of the state did not improve markedly in the second half of the 1990s, the University's general fund base continued to erode, and increases in tuition revenue offset some of the budget cuts. During these years, the University had one of the nation's largest declines (more than 25 percent) in educational appropriations per full-time student. Keeping in mind the recent large tuition increases, the administration and the governing board determined that students should not have to bear responsibility for balancing the budget due to general fund reductions. To this end there was a return to modest incremental tuition increases (3 to 5 percent). Despite little, if any, improvement in services from previous increases, minimal student protest accompanied board actions during these years. It was against this background that the next modest tuition proposal resulted in a negative board decision.

Communications and Process

The University had at least a 20-year practice of holding and accepting testimony at public hearings held across the state before making a decision on tuition. In the early years the board convened and attended these hearings, but by the end of the 1990s the administration held these meetings and board members usually did not attend. Student attendance at public hearings varied greatly from location to location and year to year. Some of the drop-off in student attendance, especially for the later years, may have reflected students' preference to give testimony only if trustees would be present to hear their concerns.

Beginning in the early 1990s, the administration initiated tuition-setting cycles with a board briefing that outlined the parameters for a tuition proposal and sought advice and guidance regarding schedules. Little, if any, feedback or substantive guidance resulted from these board briefings. The administration then prepared and distributed to students, faculty leaders, and the University community a detailed proposal that summarized the rationale for increases in the context of board tuition policy; held campus briefings; and made modifications to proposals before they were finalized. Faculty rarely commented on proposals or participated in the tuition process. The board always accepted testimony at its decision-making meetings.

Proposal Rejection Followed by Acceptance

So what changed that caused the board to reject a modest tuition proposal one spring, but accept it the following spring? The board's negative tuition vote followed several days of campus unrest and a tumultuous day of protest and testimony, much of it by minority students and community members concerned about native rights. As expected, student leaders objected to tuition increases in general. But native rights issues came to a boiling point in response to a major court decision that was handed down less than a month earlier. That decision (unrelated to the University) negated the exclusive ability of the native community to vote for leaders of a government entity established for the purpose of representing and advancing their rights.

This external event meant that a board tuition decision took place in a highly charged environment. Student leaders held an overnight protest and sleep-in at the student center and informed administrators that they could not ensure that the demonstrations to come the next day would be peaceful. This prompted the administration to take what it considered a cautionary measure of stationing state security personnel at a remote location on the campus. When this action became known to attendees during the board meeting, it added to the emotional unrest of the day.

To reach the board meeting room, trustees and administrators had to walk through a crowd of yelling people only to find their entrance blocked. They moved to another room until the route to the meeting room could be opened and made safe. The administration's tuition presentation was continually interrupted by protesting students, who then presented several hours of emotional testimony.

Adding to the confusion of the day, a list of questions from the board about tuition was shared with the administration shortly before the formal meeting. These questions touched on a wide range of subjects that for the most part asked whether other sources of revenue could be found instead of raising tuition. At the board meeting these questions were not asked.

The tuition proposal was rejected with one dissenting vote and an expression of disappointment at the behavior exhibited by some who presented testimony. In voicing their rationale for a negative vote, various board members made reference to concerns about prioritization and reallocation efforts, efficiency and productivity, native student issues, full utilization of financial aid, use of endowment funds to help with the budget crisis, the state's responsibility to fund higher education, and the need to explore all means to generate revenues before raising tuition. Two months after this board meeting, the president announced his intention to resign approximately a year later.

One year later, before his departure, the president presented to the board and they approved a nearly identical tuition proposal. Student concerns about assistance and support for native students were voiced, but not in confrontations outside of the meeting room; the volatility associated with the court ruling had subsided. Student testimonies were intense, but they were not accompanied by the same level of disruption and emotion as had occurred a year earlier.

During the course of the intervening year, the administration had worked to establish several understandings with the board. First, the matter of tuition setting and all of the emotional turmoil that went with it should not be left as one of the first things for the incoming president to decide. Second, it was well known during this time that the University regularly had end-of-the-year balances in some special and revolving funds. After the tuition rejection decision, the administration worked to explain these balances, reduced them where possible, and explained why such balances could not be substituted for tuition revenues. Third, the administration stressed that it would again hold student briefings and make every effort to respond to student concerns, but the administration could not ensure that the board's decision-making meeting would be devoid of protests. Student leaders had informed administrators that "they now knew what to do" to get the tuition matter voted down. Indeed, students attending and testifying at the meeting in which the board approved tuition increases voiced their dismay at this action because their objections were similar to those they expressed one year earlier.

Case Dynamics

What might be learned from the tuition case that would assist those practicing the art of governance? At the top of this list is the reality that, when an otherwise reasonable decision is linked negatively with an external concern that is highly political, it becomes a big issue and a wicked problem (Rittel and Webber 1973) of the highest order. External realities can overtake internal processes and result in decisions that are unexpected by all parties. It became clear that the negative tuition decision surprised board members, the administration, members of the community, political officials, and even students who had opposed increased tuition. Politically savvy boards and administrators recognize when external events beyond their control turn a routine/bureaucratic matter into a big, messy issue, and together they consider strategies to deal with the situation.

Decisions on divisive big issues are particularly difficult for trustees/regents. The lay members of these bodies serve as volunteers for the public good. They do not like making decisions in highly charged and emotional environments, especially decisions that place them in opposition to students, the very population whose education they are committed to advance. Emotional testimony from students makes boards uncomfortable and even reluctant to take actions that otherwise they would judge to be reasonable. Understanding a decision's context is key to the art of governance.

When a big issue is on the table, the amount of detailed information provided during consultation processes and the length of these processes will not ensure a well-informed audience. No matter how early the process starts or how much time is allowed for discussion and clarification, full engagement in the substance of the matter by many constituents and board members often comes only shortly before decision making is scheduled. *This means that a diverse group of players is attempting to absorb a great deal of complex information in a very short time.* For the vast majority of routine/bureaucratic actions that involve minimal opposition, this is not a problem. When the matter turns into a big issue, last-minute engagement creates an environment in which one or two pieces of information, the presence or absence of one or two key decision makers, or the statements of a few individuals committed to supporting or opposing the action can determine the outcome.

All comments and observations shared with a decision-making body as they are about to take a vote on a big issue tend to carry the same weight, as there is no time for a proper analysis of concerns. Administrators are often reluctant to publicly confront or embarrass those who oppose an action by saying they are misrepresenting the facts. As a result, decision makers are left to sort out informed concerns from those that have little basis in fact or relevance to the issue before them. Most governing board members do not anticipate being placed in such a position and may feel that this reality means they were not well served by the administration. It can also mean that decision makers may not have taken advantage of earlier briefings and explanations for the proposed action. All parties to an event that has the potential to become messy have a responsibility to be prepared for highly charged emotional environments in which civility may not prevail.

Decision-making bodies that are bound by sunshine laws have additional difficulty sorting out last-minute emotional pleas. In the tuition case, the board recessed before its negative vote, only to be told by its legal counsel that they could not discuss among themselves any of the issues raised. Returning to the open meeting, a board member expressed poignant support for the students, and this quickly became the position of all but one member of the board present.

In a highly polarized and political environment, the rationale provided for rejecting a proposal tends to be global in nature and extremely difficult to refute immediately. For example, in the tuition case, board concerns could be summed up as follows: the institution should propose tuition increases when no other sources of revenue are available. Because it could be argued that any large and complex system of higher education can always find some additional revenues (by halting any number of research, instructional, or administrative activities), it would be nearly impossible to increase tuition at any time. When global issues of this sort emerge, all parties to the process have a responsibility to delay or suggest reconsideration of an action until conflicting information can be clarified, the rationale can be sharpened, and the matter can be taken up in as calm an atmosphere as possible.

If possible, most faculty will avoid involvement in a controversial big issue such as tuition. If they support a tuition increase, they risk alienating students. If they publicly oppose such an increase while making the case that their work is not being adequately funded, they lose credibility. The safer route is to be silent, to comment on some specific aspect of a proposal, or to agree that additional revenues are needed but maintain that the institution or the state should provide them from other sources.

Those on the "winning" side of a big-issue outcome will feel empowered and confident that they know how to influence future decisions. This is especially the case if the final decision is not the action recommended by the administration. The message student leaders took away from the negative tuition decision was that, if they could bypass the administration and go directly to the board with their concerns, they could turn back a major administrative recommendation that they did not like. In this context, contrary decisions made at a later time are interpreted as an unwillingness to listen to the opposition. For example, in the tuition case, the day after trustees voted *for* a tuition increase, the student newspaper accused the board of failing to hear student testimonies; the paper expressed dismay that the board would approve a tuition increase despite what was described as a public outcry, tears, and even begging—all of which was similar to what had occurred the year before.

Finally, trustees and others in such positions often do not realize that a negative decision on a big issue weakens the administration's capacity to govern. After the negative tuition decision, the administration and the board had different perceptions of the long-term impact of the board's action. Trustees were concerned about the impact on individuals, namely, that members of the administration understand that the board appreciated and respected their work. It was difficult for some trustees to understand the administration's perception that a public split between the board and the administration on such a big issue would convey a lack of confidence in the administration's capacity to govern and signal that it was time for a new administration. Keeping an institution focused on common goals requires a partnership between governing boards and the administration. Board and administration orientation sessions that address (independent of specific issues) the ramifications of public disagreements are critical.

EXTERNAL FORCES

The tuition case has illustrated the impact of external political events on internal governance. We will return to other lessons learned from this case in Chapter 7. Now, we turn to other profound forces that impact the governance process.

An earlier analysis of shared authority began with the assumption that the basis of authority and legitimacy for academic governance required reexamination as the result of a push by students, administrators, trustees, and unions for a greater share in the authority that historically was the domain of "faculty power" (Mortimer and McConnell 1978). Now, more than 25 years later, we continue the focus on the authority and legitimacy of academic governance, but place this examination in the larger context of societal forces—demographic, economic, and political—that go beyond those exerted by any one group of participants.

The higher education literature has for some time routinely discussed various perspectives on the proposition articulated by the Pew Higher Education Roundtable in 1993: "The changes most important to the university are those that are external to it. What is new is the use of societal demand—in the American context, market forces—to reshape the university." Pew added a corollary to this proposition, namely, "The failure to understand these changes puts the university at risk" (Pew 1993, 1A). In 1998, the Association of Governing Boards of Universities and Colleges (AGB) stated: "The world is changing faster than the governance system can accommodate" and went on to wonder whether governing boards could act effectively in this environment or might be bypassed altogether (AGB 1998, 9). In 2001, AGB added that "inappropriate external influences on a governing board have great potential to skew an institution's priorities and compromise its capacity to serve the public interest" (AGB 2001, 6). In a similar vein, the work of Frank Newman and his Futures Project staff colleagues discussed at length unstoppable and ubiquitous forces reshaping higher education and forcing institutions to behave as competitors (Newman, Couturier, and Scurry 2004). Benjamin and Carroll (1998) have argued that changes in the environment require restructuring higher education governance systems.

It is not our intention here to do what others have expertly done, namely, analyze or provide a comprehensive literature review of the many external forces reshaping American higher education. For example, Zemsky, Wegner, and Massy (2005) provide an excellent analysis of external forces; Blustain, Goldstein, and Lozier (1999) contribute an assessment of higher education's new competitive landscape; Gregorian (2005) provides a concise summary of challenges facing universities; and Gumport and Pusser (1997) address calls for reform and academic restructuring.

Drawing on selected works and our experience, we make the case that market forces have affected the debates about the legitimacy of the partners' roles in internal governance. To establish the context within which shared governance arrangements unfold, we begin with a discussion of the role and limitations of the market in framing higher education policy and go on to discuss a set of forces that place strains on the university's longstanding ways of doing business and present particular challenges for shared governance. These include:

- The rising importance of forces that are particularly market related:
    - The changing nature of student populations,
    - The globalization of science and technology,
    - The increased importance of educational technology, and
    - The increased emphasis on educational accountability;

- The increasing volatility of state- and system-level actions; and
- The integration of the university into the larger society.

Each of these forces is important in itself, but their cumulative impact is transforming the higher education enterprise and requires a better understanding by boards, administrators, and faculty of how the political model influences their shared participation in governance.

The Market and Higher Education Policy

The analysts at the National Center for Public Policy and Higher Education (1998) point out that market forces are not new to higher education. What is different is the capacity of cumulative market forces to replace public policy as a means of expressing public needs. Within higher education the power of the market is evident in the competition for students, money, and prestige. Kirp (2003) expresses the same theme: "What *is* new, and troubling, is the raw power that money directly exerts over so many aspects of higher education" (3). This raw power can have negative or positive ramifications: "market forces lead some schools to forget that they are not simply businesses while turning others into stronger, better places" (7).

The analysts at the National Center for Higher Education Management Systems (NCHEMS) share a number of concerns that unfold from an excessive reliance on market-driven phenomena as an *exclusive* framework for setting policies. For example, the market tends to emphasize higher education as a private rather than a public good, and this leads to the corollary that individuals benefit more than society and therefore should pay the greater share of costs (Jones, Ewell, and McGuinness 1998, 19–20).

Public or institutional higher education policymakers would be well advised to recognize that the issue is about the *imperfections* of the marketplace rather than an either/or question. For example, rather than engage in the debate about whether higher education is a private or public good, it would be more useful for governance partners to recognize that it is both and to focus attention on the more critical issue of who should receive the subsidies. In this case, the starting point is recognition that all students, certainly those in the not-for-profit sector, are subsidized. Massy (2003, 75) points out that even full-pay students at private institutions are heavily subsidized. In their discussion of stratification in American higher education, McPherson and Schapiro (1998, 99 and 142–143) note that, for all students, educational costs exceed tuition. Subsidies in the form of the difference between what the average student actually pays and average institutional educational expenditures plus financial assistance is greater at institutions that typically attract more affluent students (public and private research universities) and lower at institutions that tend to attract lower-income students (two-year publics).

The public policy issue is who gets the subsidies. Here we know that, just as in the larger society, the imperfections of the market impact some populations more severely than others. Most analysts agree that market mechanisms tend not to work at all for students who need basic skills or those who traditionally under-participate in higher education, namely, low-income and at-risk students. As a matter of public priorities, many economists and analysts believe that the at-risk populations should receive the greatest, not the least, subsidies.

Governing boards and administrators should be concerned about the cases in which higher education holds a monopoly on "the ticket to the good life." For place-bound students and those whose affordability quotient is very low, local public community colleges and universities are their only realistic options for benefiting from higher education. It can reasonably be said that, for these populations, the local college holds a monopoly on the "ticket" that leads to the increased lifetime earnings and benefits associated with postsecondary education. For example, in the state of Hawai'i, the University of Hawai'i is the only public university available and enrolls approximately 75 percent of all college students in the state. Many of these are underrepresented populations, and the campuses of the university system provide them the broadest opportunity for a postsecondary education. Yet, in our experience, it can be a recurring challenge to persuade some members of the university community, the public, and even legislators that tuition rates and financial aid packages, especially at the public two-year campuses, must reflect the larger institutional commitment to higher education access and not necessarily market-place tuition rates. It takes mission-centered and politically savvy boards and administrators to juggle these realities and to develop sound tuition-setting policy in such environments.

At the same time, effective and efficient markets assume a competitive environment, a condition that does not exist where higher education has a monopoly. In the polity, monopolies are often limited or controlled by public regulations. Newman and colleagues point out that, in some cases, there may be a need for some regulation in the higher education context. What is to be avoided is excessive reliance on market forces that result in a two-tiered system, with traditional high-quality institutions reserved for an elite class and other institutions serving nontraditional or disadvantaged students. There can also be a concern that the quality and scope of academic offerings will decline as institutions focus more on profitability and less on delivering high-quality, often expensive products (Newman, Couturier, and Scurry 2004, 81–103). In our experience high-quality, expensive education is often what is needed to serve the nontraditional or disadvantaged students who can least afford it.

We agree with Newman and colleagues that market forces have invaded higher education and will not diminish; they influence higher education policy. It is up to higher education to determine how this influence unfolds. At a minimum, governance processes must ensure that the public purposes of higher education are not subverted while responding to legitimate market forces. Newman and colleagues eloquently stated these purposes as "teaching that is nonideological, research that is open and trustworthy, and service that helps address the difficult issues that society faces" (Newman, Couturier, and Scurry 2004, 214). To these purposes we would add access to higher education opportunity and a reasonable chance at success by the neediest students.

The Market and Students

Those interested in an in-depth treatment of higher education demographics will find Keller's (2001, 219–235) analysis enlightening, as he discusses the impact of declining birth rates, an aging and more educated American population, the massive numbers of immigrants, and changes in family structures. The cumulative effects of these and other changes in student markets make the resulting trends of great importance for the future of the academy and influence arguments about the legitimate responsibilities of the governance partners.

For example, our experience with the marketplace of providers reinforces the observations of Newman and colleagues that traditional institutions no longer hold a monopoly for some levels of education, especially high-demand professional programs. This means that students have multiple and different choices and can be more demanding and sophisticated (Newman, Couturier, and Scurry 2004, 16–18). Kirp (2003, 16–20) refers to the competition for students in marketing terms not commonly used in higher education—"trolling for students: the bait" and "pricing the product." Students have a growing interest in convenience and effectiveness, and a readiness to attend multiple institutions on the way to a degree. Our experience at a research university revealed that only 30 percent of those receiving diplomas had the *single undergraduate campus* experience that very likely was common among administrators, senior faculty, and community leaders. Also, attendance *at the same time at two or more campuses* in the university system, although not pervasive, was a reality (University of Hawai'i 2004). Faculty accustomed to students starting and completing at their campus can be rather astonished when some wonder: "Whose degree is it, anyway?"

Alongside this mobility factor is the reality of a remarkable growth in the U.S. postsecondary student population. College attendance has become the norm for high school completers in the United States, 65 percent of whom enroll in college, and about 80 percent of undergraduate enrollments are in the public sector (Mortenson 2001 and 2003). The higher education experience is not yet universal, but it is moving in that direction. If we accept Trow's (1996) premise that mass education refers to a system that educates 15 percent of an age cohort, the United States, with an overall participation rate of more than 26 percent, has provided mass education for at least three decades (Currie et al. 2003, 25).

As more and more students enroll and higher education moves from elite systems to systems of mass and even universal higher education, we have noted a concern that quality suffers. For example, this view is expressed, as we have heard it, in the assumption of a de facto diminution in quality when traditional content areas are offered on campuses where some student educational goals tend to be credentials in occupational or preprofessional fields. This view leads to serious divisions within faculty ranks when student transfer issues are on the table. These divisions test shared governance and can lead to serious faculty/administrative splits as administrators are perceived to have chosen the wrong side.

For example, when institutional commitments to access are combined with the reality of more students and more mobile students, the result is ever larger numbers of students who have expectations that credits received at one institution should transfer to other institutions. These expectations have ramifications for one of the fundamental tenets of shared governance, namely, the faculty's legitimate claim for exclusive control over their institution's curriculum. In the student transfer case discussed in Chapter 4, we will see how efforts to facilitate degree attainment by mobile student populations within a multicampus system can become a big, messy governance issue.

The Market and Globalization

The globalization of science and technology is a fact of life. "The technological revolution that is sweeping the world today is powered less by harnessing new sources of energy and mechanical invention and more by advances in applied science and engineering" (Slaughter and Leslie 1997, 26). This revolution depends on universities to train increasing numbers of professionals "employed by corporations to invent, maintain, and innovate with regard to sophisticated technologies and products" (27).

In coining the term *academic capitalism*, Slaughter and Leslie refer to the impact of institutional and professorial markets or market-like behavior designed to secure external funding. They observe that one of the major changes is that faculty used to be situated between capital and labor, but now are positioned squarely in the marketplace. For example, before the 1980s, biology was a basic science funded by national governments through competitive processes. By the mid 1980s, most full professors of molecular biology held equity positions in spin-off companies. Slaughter and Leslie point out that there is strong evidence that state and national governments *expect* intellectual property to be a significant factor in driving their economies. They "increasingly see faculty work as possible intellectual property, more valuable in global markets as product or commodity than as unremunerated contributions to an international community of scholars" (Slaughter and Leslie 1997, 4–8 and 36–39).

As external forces encourage higher education to devote more resources to creating and managing innovations, universities structure their intellectual property policies to take advantage of the resulting financial opportunities. These and other global trends tend to privilege those sectors of the academy more closely linked to the market, especially science and technology fields, over the traditional liberal arts. Market-related disciplines offer faculty more opportunities to benefit personally from the commercialization of innovations. And governments may direct a larger share of a dwindling higher education pie to fields judged to be more directly supportive of a competitive economy. One result is that competition within the university for available resources becomes intense. These realities drive divisions within faculty ranks and test the legitimacy of faculty senates that are unable to articulate positions representative of the entire faculty on issues dealing with intellectual property and academic freedom. For example, a recent debate at the University of Hawai'i over whether to permit the U.S. Navy to build a research laboratory on campus revealed a rift between arts and humanities faculty and those in the sciences. The scientific researchers see defense money as just another source of support and viewed the resolution passed by the campus faculty senate opposing the laboratory as an indication that academic freedom is a monopoly of the majority (Field 2006).

In another case, the higher education community was stunned when the plant-biology department at the University of California-Berkeley agreed to a "strategic alliance" with Novartis, a multinational life-sciences company. This multiyear agreement illustrated the tightening relationships between multinational corporations and universities in the basic battle for economic resources. In exchange for substantial funding and access to proprietary technologies, the Berkeley department agreed to provide Novartis with differential access for licensing purposes to about one-third of its research discoveries. This arrangement resulted in substantial debate and criticism within the higher education community—some worried about the public interest in such arrangements and others about the danger of warping the direction of departmental research. To the relief of some, the Berkeley arrangement with Novartis was not renewed. Clark Kerr was quoted as saying that he was "much more concerned about Novartis II and Novartis III" (Blumenstyk 1998 and 2001).

We suggest that the forces of globalization will result in more and more "big issues" that will strain the fabric of shared governance and bring the politics of advocacy (a topic discussed in greater detail in Chapter 2) into play within faculty ranks as well as among faculty, administrators, and boards. Currie et al. (2003, 196–197) present two future university scenarios for dealing with globalization: (1) adapt to external forces, either through acquiescence or manipulation, in order to survive; or (2) resist and survive practices that are harmful to the essence of the university in order to preserve the academy. Agreement on how to implement either of these scenarios will require not just politically savvy administrators, but politically savvy faculty leaders with many of the skills and talents we discuss in Chapter 7.

The Market and Technology

In a 1999 interview, Clark Kerr, president-emeritus of the University of California and former head of the Carnegie Council on Policy Studies, observed that, "for 500 years, higher education hasn't faced much technological change. Almost everything else—agriculture, industry, and any other sector you can think of—has been affected much more by technological change than we have" (Ikenberry 1999, 14). This situation has changed dramatically. Any higher education professional whose career has spanned 20 years, and in some cases fewer, can remember doing business without the Internet, e-mail, personal computers, on-line purchasing and student registration, distance learning, cell phones, and a myriad of other technological changes. In its instructional mission alone, the importance of technology threatens higher education's traditional monopoly over content. The emerging information technologies have removed the constraints that space and time place on teaching and learning activities (Duderstadt 1999). Arthur Levine's example is intriguing.

> As for content, the story of Microsoft and the Encyclopedia Britannica is instructive. Bill Gates invited the most eminent of encyclopedias to develop a CD-Rom edition. Britannica turned him down worried about losing the market for its traditional hard copy edition. So Microsoft bought Funk and Wagnalls and turned it into the digital *Encarta*. In less than two years, *Encarta* was the best selling encyclopedia in the world. Britannica sales plummeted. They went back to Microsoft and were told they would now have to pay to put their encyclopedia online. The lesson is that if distributors, like Microsoft, are unable to get content providers to join them, they may well buy the content or develop the capacity to create content themselves. (Levine 2000)

The lesson here is that the profit potential for those who are content producers is remarkable if the content can be adapted to emerging technologies. This profit potential will attract newcomers to the "content market," challenging higher education's traditional monopoly and furthering the previously reported market and global trends impacting higher education. Interested readers will find enlightening Katz's treatment of the challenges posed by the combined pressures of competition and information technology. In particular, he argues that institutions will be impelled to rethink their instructional products and markets and deal with a host of sensitive campus and public policy issues. "Higher education, as both a major supplier and consumer of information resources, can neither sit this dance out nor wait to be asked" (Katz 1999, 35).

A reference to intellectual property debates at the University of Hawai'i can illustrate changes that higher education is facing in dealing with issues of intellectual property and content. More than 4,000 faculty are covered by a systemwide collective bargaining agreement at the University of Hawai'i. That agreement has an intellectual property clause. It gives the faculty a substantial share of patent and license royalties and fees resulting from inventions in University laboratories. The University owns the patents, but it shares the revenues that accrue from any commercialization of the product. However, problems arise in defining the nature of academic work in an institution with a variety of academics. Some of the faculty teach at community colleges and, although they have scholarly responsibilities, typically they are not heavily involved in original research. The faculty at the regional campuses participate in various forms of research and scholarship, but the organized research functions of the university system are embodied in a 2,400-member faculty at the research campus. At this campus there are some faculty and professional staff whose only responsibility is research, and there are others, like extension agents and faculty specialists, who provide services to a variety of agencies and clients. The largest share of faculty at this and the other campuses are expected to teach, do research, and provide service.

It is fairly clear that, when a patent comes out of one of the University's laboratories, the University can patent it and share the appropriate royalties with the faculty member. It is less clear who owns the product when it involves release time for a faculty member assigned to develop a course for distance education. The euphemism is often "a work for hire." The University, of course, maintains that products developed as the result of release time should be owned by the party who pays for that release time, the University. Not surprisingly, the faculty union argues that the product is no different from that produced by a faculty member in humanities who copyrights a book and keeps the royalties. A complicating factor is involved in the case of faculty who use significant University resources to develop products. These might be software products that require substantial institutional computing resources or electronic courses that require significant staff support. In either case the use of University resources can be major, and the question then arises as to who owns the property or the software.

There is probably no better example of the challenges faced by traditional shared governance mechanisms than those inherent in debates about intellectual property. How are the interests of all parties reconciled when the quality of a product is not dependent primarily or exclusively on the intellect of one individual, but on the intellectual expertise and talents of faculty and highly trained staff, and on sophisticated technology, classroom, and laboratory resources that might otherwise be used to enhance other important institutional priorities such as learning and living spaces for students and libraries? In sum, we agree with Katz (1999, 42–48) that realizing the resource potential associated with extending technology-enriched instructional programs requires addressing the sensitive issue of who owns the distribution and sale rights to an institution's instructional materials and collections.

The Market and Accountability

The market demands responsiveness and results—accountability. In higher education these demands get formalized by government officials, governing boards, and accrediting agencies who pass laws, formulate policies, or dictate standards that require institutional leaders and their faculties to document institutional performance, demonstrate educational effectiveness, and assess student learning. A new vocabulary has emerged, with terms such as *educational outcomes, performance measures, benchmarks, performance funding strategies,* and *accountability for student learning.*

More and more students take courses or even entire degree programs in a virtual environment, attend multiple institutions, and return to higher education throughout their lives to pursue new skills. As these and other conditions for student learning and patterns of student attendance change, they are forcing changes in how higher education must demonstrate quality.

A common generalization is that traditional provider-centric measures of quality such as the award of degrees, even by prestigious institutions, are not adequate in a client- and market-centered environment. The perception is that the degree (especially the baccalaureate degree) does not certify a common standard of attainment. Therefore institutions are encouraged to certify learning and award degrees based on demonstrated competence in clearly specified areas. Another reason for this shift is the reality that almost two-thirds of the students who graduate from colleges attend multiple institutions. As the analysts at NCHEMS note: "Restricting quality-assurance mechanisms to the individual 'nodes' in the chain of instruction—rather than focusing on the collective experience and its consequences—misses key aspects of the quality-assurance problem as a whole" (Jones, Ewell, and McGuinness 1998, 14–15).

The debate about what constitutes quality in higher education all too often drives wedges between the major partners in shared governance. Administrators are pressured to respond to boards, legislators, federal and private agencies, and the community with data that demonstrate ever-improving student participation and performance, institutional affordability, and significant economic impact on the community. Faculty may tolerate such measures, but rightfully argue that the impact on society of what happens in their classrooms cannot be readily measured by graduation and retention rates or even professional licensing exams. It can take years for a quality college education to bear fruit. Some will argue that the national accountability movement can get sidetracked by measuring everything that moves; others say that improved assessment should be used to create change, not simply to record it.

The adaptations needed to achieve a balanced approach to accountability will be troublesome to the academy. Faculty are frustrated when the public asks questions such as: How can higher education serve us better? They prefer the question: How can society be made to recognize and support the value of what we do? External and internal actors lament the extent to which governance processes are not designed to provide answers to these differing perceptions and expectations.

In summary, the new accountability environment is forcing faculty and administrators to come together and replace educational quality judgments based on credentials and prestige with measures that demonstrate knowledge and skills actually acquired—to move from attendance to success. The need for this joint faculty-administration effort was recognized by educational leaders participating in the 2006 Commission on the Future of Higher Education when they noted that their recommendations would have to win over college administrators and faculty who ultimately have to "do much of the heavy lifting" (Lederman 2006). As the student transfer case will demonstrate, heavy lifting requires faculty and administrative leaders who are sufficiently politically savvy to understand and appreciate that they can make the accountability environment work for the betterment of their institutions, students, and the public good while maintaining their integrity. We agree with Trow's assessment that "accountability depends on truth-telling ... creating a system ... that does not punish truth-telling and reward the appearance of achievement" (1996, 314).

State and System Level Governance

Changes in state government policies and practices for higher education require constant monitoring by institutional actors. According to experienced observers, fundamental shifts point to renegotiation of the social contract between higher education and state government (Breneman 2004; Longanecker 2006; McGuinness 2003; Wellman 2006). We have referred to many of these shifts in the foregoing discussion of external forces. They include:

- A shift from a focus on providers (institutions) to a focus on clients (learners);
- A shift from centralized regulation and control to decentralized management and the use of incentives, performance funding, and consumer information;
- A shift from institutional subsidies to competitive awards;
- A shift from accountability focused on institutional performance to accountability for the educational attainment of the state's population;
- The increased pressure for higher education to be a key driver for a competitive state economy;
- The increasing influence of alternative, for-profit institutions; and
- The increased politicization of governing boards.

As we will illustrate in the school closure case in Chapter 3, these shifts can be accompanied by mixed signals. Some of the volatility in big issues that administrators and faculty attempt to deal with (for example, the reallocation of resources or restructuring of programs) comes about when government leaders express opposite points of view. Some may say privately that an institution should have taken proposed actions sooner; others argue publicly that the proposed actions should not be taken at all. And all too often such conflict occurs when the needs of the state outstrip the resources available.

Over the past 25 years, there have been fundamental changes in state structures and often attempts at improper political intrusions. State higher education systems now encompass the vast majority of public campuses and enroll millions of students. Three states have planning/service agencies, and roughly half of the rest have governing boards and half have coordinating boards (McGuinness 2002 and 2003; Newman 1987; Fretwell 2000). Because this book's concern is for campus governance, we will not argue the merits of governing versus coordinating boards or the dynamics of their operation. These vary depending on the conditions and context of the separate states. Our concern is the influence/control or impact these structures have on campus governance.

Here the evidence is troubling. According to McGuinness (2003, 3), "the disjuncture between higher education and state leaders is not that states don't care; it is that they care about agendas different from those that drive institutional behaviors." Longanecker (2006, 112–113) summarizes this disjuncture by questioning whether existing governance structures can serve the public good in the future as well as they have in the past given the increasing weight placed on public interests and needs and a resource-constrained environment; he suggests that governance structures must evolve to fit new realities.

There is also great concern among institutional stakeholders about attempts by state and system officials to intrude improperly in campus affairs. Newman (1987, 1–3) recognizes the difference between appropriate public policy questions and inappropriate political intrusions. Inappropriate intrusion is characterized by attempts to interfere with the operation of the university, either to serve ends that are questionable or to serve ends that may or may not be questionable through means that are questionable. There are three forms of such intrusion: bureaucratic, political, and ideological. Bureaucratic intrusions, the most common form, simply reflect the accumulated weight of unnecessary or counterproductive regulations. Political intrusion—the exercise of raw political power—is an important factor in some states. Ideological intrusion includes attempts to impact university activity through control of the curriculum or limits on intellectual freedom. Politically savvy partners in shared governance are challenged to interpret and sort these external influences and devise appropriate responses that protect academic freedom and basic institutional purposes with minimal disruption to the pipeline of resources the institution needs to flourish. For example, when the Pennsylvania legislature recently held hearings to investigate whether public institutions in the state indoctrinate students in left-wing ideology, Temple University provided a measured response—streamlining grievance procedures and making sure students are aware of them (Jacobson 2006).

System-level bureaucracies add complexity to this pattern of external influences on campus-level shared governance practices. Systems often have the responsibility to appoint presidents; allocate resources among campuses; determine campus size, scope, and mission; audit campus finances; mediate disputes between campuses; and represent and advocate for the entire system before the public, the governor, and the legislature. In many systems, such as the University of California, system guidelines determine the structure and processes of shared governance at the campus level. In cases of system collective bargaining with faculty, these matters actually may be determined at the system, not the campus level, a subject to which we return in Chapter 2.

Integration of the University and Society

When considered in combination—market impacts on policy, the changing nature of student populations, globalization, technological innovation, pressures to be accountable, and volatility in state government—these external forces create greater dependency between the university and society. In considering the future of the university, Clark Kerr observed:

> In the sixties, I talked about the "multiversity," but if I were writing today, I
> might use the term "integrated university." Integrated into society. Integrated
> into the military efforts of the nation. Integrated into health care and the
> legal system. I talked about how we were reaching out in many ways, but
> society was also moving in on us. Higher education now faces the challenge
> of being less of an independent force and being integrated into more elements
> of society than ever before. (Ikenberry 1999, 19)

Integration into society means universities can no longer be self-contained
entities. Engagement means opening institutions to external influences while
insisting that the world beyond the campus respect the imperatives of the university (Kellogg Commission 1999, 39). Maintaining such duality is difficult, if not
impossible. Engagement can reduce the amount of autonomy enjoyed by institutions and professors in the areas of research and development, curricula, and
access (Slaughter and Leslie 1997, 222–226). Engagement can also provide the
opportunity for higher education to use its governance of areas such as the curriculum and program administration to bring its considerable resources to bear on
societal problems. The challenge is to adapt internal governance processes to deal
with the changed nature of the university's external environment while remaining
responsive to mission. The institutional mission should be clear and well understood by all institutional stakeholders and should encourage decisions that are
consistent with public needs and the institutional agenda. What must be avoided
is a drifting away from the fundamental nature of higher education and its basic
missions of research, teaching, and service. Zemsky and Massy (1995) argue for a
partnership between the core—the home of liberal arts and undergraduates—and
the entrepreneurial perimeter of the institution.

A large part of the remainder of this book responds to this simple question:
How can the university adapt its internal governance processes to deal with the
changed nature of its environment while remaining responsive to its mission?
For the most part, internal university constituents are not prepared to give legitimacy to market control of the university's decision-making processes—they are
not prepared to let money be the coin of the realm. Kirp suggests that, lacking a
"principled defense of nonmarket values," higher education may degenerate into
just another business. He makes the persuasive case that the critical question is
whether there is "anyone with sufficient stature to persuade the public that, at
their best, institutions of higher learning offer something of such great value that
the enterprise is worth subsidizing, even in the face of market pressures?" (Kirp
2005, 127). We suggest that it takes boards, administrators, and faculty working
together to make the case that their institutions are first and foremost houses of
learning. We do not dispute the importance of institutions understanding their
"clients" and their multiple markets. Understand, for example, that there is not
one student body on most campuses, there are several. Some of them are prepared
to pursue college degrees and others are not. Some can afford to study full time,
but many cannot. There is not one state economic agenda, there are many, and
there are many publics—some demanding support for a particular industry and

others for the environment and the cultural priorities of the community. To do all of these things while not losing sight of core values requires a team effort; it requires shared governance that works.

The Kellogg Commission (1999, 1), in an open letter to university leaders, asserted that given the evidence of campus resources and superbly qualified professors and staff, "we can organize our institutions to serve both local and national needs in a more coherent and effective way." We would add to this admonition that we can also *govern our institutions in ways that are less divisive, more unifying, and supportive of institutional missions and societal needs.*

SUMMARY

The charge to be mission-centered, market-smart, *and* politically savvy sets the stage for our analysis of campus governance. The tuition case helped illustrate how the governance process becomes complicated and how unexpected consequences emerge when external factors overtake internal governance processes. An understanding of the external forces discussed in this chapter helps establish the larger world context for the governance challenges facing higher education. Governments, businesses, and private entities that award grants and contract for services, the competition for students, the demands of a mobile student population, heightened global competition, and employers who demand workers trained in entry-level skills—these are all examples of how the market places demands on higher education governance structures. The admonition to be politically savvy is easier said than done and requires a consideration of the role of power and influence in shared governance, a subject to which we now turn.

CHAPTER

Shared Governance, Politics, and the Role of Senates and Unions

> There is a "kind of lawlessness" in any large university, with many separate sources of initiative and power; and the task is to keep this lawlessness within reasonable bounds.
>
> —Clark Kerr, *The Uses of the University*

In Chapter 1 the issue of tuition setting illustrated the governance context at one institution and set the background for a discussion of the external forces that impinge on governance in general. In this chapter, we turn to the dynamics of governance *within* the campus as it seeks to deal with a volatile set of forces.

Various authors have provided excellent literature reviews and treatments of the history, perceptions, and practices of shared governance in higher education (a sample includes Eckel 2000; Eckel and Kezar 2003; Hines 2000; Miller and Caplow 2003; Mortimer and McConnell 1978; Rosser 2002). Kezar and Eckel (2004) provide a comprehensive synthesis of scholarly perspectives on governance, and Tierney and Lechuga (2004) offer competing conceptions of shared governance. It is not our intention to review these and other works, but rather to draw on selected literature that helps us analyze the many separate sources of initiative and power that are part of a shared governance environment. We also expand on our earlier discussion of shared governance claims when big issues are at stake and when collective bargaining is a factor (Mortimer and Sathre 2006, 79–80 and 85–91).

We begin by reviewing the cultural tradition of shared governance as the ideal type and contrast it with the way it is practiced. We show that there are fundamental disagreements within the academy about what shared governance actually means and how it should be implemented. These disagreements are amplified when an institution is faced with very important or big issues.

On the big issues, conflict is normal and goals are ambiguous and contested. In these situations, political values trump those of shared governance and increase the legitimacy attributed to the rules of advocacy. We believe that understanding when and how political values come into play and honing the skills it takes to deal with them are the heart of the art of governance.

This chapter continues by discussing faculty senates and unions as the principal vehicles for faculty-administrative interaction at the campus level. We conclude by showing how jurisdictional conflicts between senates and unions have been articulated.

THE DEBATE ABOUT SHARED GOVERNANCE

In recent years there have been several national discussions regarding the adequacy of prevailing statements about shared governance. The standard shared governance reference is the American Association of University Professors (AAUP), *Policy Documents and Reports,* 2001. The "Red Book," as this compilation is commonly referred to, contains reports and documents on a wide range of topics relevant to governance, including 28 statements on academic freedom, tenure, and due process. There are more than 30 other statements on such matters as professional ethics, research and training, collective bargaining, and student rights. Of interest to us here are nine statements on "College and University Government."

The statement on government jointly formulated in the 1960s by the AAUP, the American Council on Education (ACE), and the Association of Governing Boards (AGB) provides the basis for the widespread acceptance of shared authority as the ideal to be achieved. It is the standard institutional reference for desirable academic governance policy. This joint statement is "a call to mutual understanding regarding the government of colleges and universities" based on a community of interest among inescapably interdependent parties—the governing board, administration, faculty, students, and others. This interdependence requires "adequate communication among these components and full opportunity for appropriate joint planning and effort." The statement recognizes that "joint efforts in an academic institution will take a variety of forms," but it asserts that two general conclusions are warranted: "(1) important areas of action involve at one time or another the initiating capacity and decision-making participation of all the institutional components, and (2) differences in the weight of each voice, from one point to the next, should be determined by reference to the responsibility of each component for the particular matter at hand" (AAUP 2001, 218).

Recognizing that the governing board has final institutional authority, "the joint statement recommends sharing authority among the constituents of a college or university on the understanding that some areas of decision making require joint endeavor and that others are essentially separate jurisdictions in which one constituent has primary, but not exclusive responsibility" (Mortimer and McConnell 1978, 6). For example, the joint AAUP, ACE, and AGB statement notes that the board plays a central role in managing the endowment, obtaining needed capital and operating funds, and in broad personnel policy. Areas that require joint efforts among the board, administration, and faculty include long-range planning, decisions on buildings and facilities, resource allocation, and short- and long-range priorities. The faculty have primary responsibility (defined in the joint statement as "the ability to take action which has the force of legislation and can be overruled only in rare instances and for compelling reasons stated in detail") for the curriculum, subject matter and methods of instruction, research, faculty status, and areas of student life that relate to the educational process. In these areas the power of review or final decision lodged in the governing board is to be exercised adversely only in exceptional cases and for reasons communicated to the faculty (AAUP 2001, 218–221).

In a separate but supportive statement, The Higher Education Program and Policy Council of the American Federation of Teachers (AFT) sets forth six principles of shared governance:

- Faculty and professional staff set academic standards and curriculum;
- Faculty and professional staff require academic freedom;
- Faculty and professional staff should have primacy on academic personnel and status;
- Participation in shared governance should be expanded;
- Unions, representative assemblies, and faculty senates all can have significant roles in shared governance; and
- Accrediting agencies should support fully the concept of shared governance in their standards. (AFT 2002, 7–9)

We conclude from the responsibilities outlined in the AFT principles and the joint AAUP, ACE, and AGB statement summarized previously that there is a broad consensus on the basic ideals on which shared governance should rest. A different emphasis, however, is found in the AGB *Statement on Institutional Governance*, which is expressed as seven principles:

- The ultimate responsibility for the institution rests with the board;
- The board has ultimate responsibility and full authority to determine institutional mission; it is responsible for establishing strategic directions by insisting on the participation of stakeholders in comprehensive planning;
- Even though the profit motive does not typically apply, colleges and universities have many of the characteristics of corporations, and their managerial and business affairs should pay appropriate attention to commonly accepted business standards;
- Governing boards should model the behavior they expect of other participants in governance;
- The board is responsible for establishing the rules by which the voices of diverse internal stakeholders—nonacademic staff, part-time and adjunct faculty, and students—may be heard;
- Board members have the responsibility to serve the institution as a whole and not particular constituencies; and

- System or multicampus boards have the duty to clarify the responsibilities of system and campus heads and any institutional quasi-governing or advisory bodies.
  (AGB 1999, 3–6)

The AGB statements seem to reflect more of a business/corporate set of assumptions about governance (e.g., authority can be delegated, but the board's responsibilities cannot). Although the faculty are important, the board must account for
the views of students and other internal stakeholders. Corporate standards should
be used to govern managerial and business affairs. But as illustrated in the following
AFT statement, faculty associations typically contest assumptions associated with
the notion that colleges and universities ought to be run more like businesses.

> Because an ever-growing number of board members and administrators with
> this mindset have reached positions of responsibility on campus, a direct assault
> is being launched on the practice of shared governance in higher education.
> There is a feeling … that any sharing of authority impedes their "right" to
> make the big decisions. They believe they know what is best and that faculty
> and staff should step aside and let the managers take charge. (AFT 2002, 3)

In our view, reconciling these seemingly competing claims for primacy in governance requires an assessment of the adequacy of shared governance arrangements. Our observations on this subject are shared as we analyze case study
dynamics throughout this book. For the interested reader, a few references that
give attention to shared governance arrangements include Birnbaum (2004),
CHEPA (2003), Duderstadt and Womack (2003), Gayle, Tewarie, and White
(2003), Gerber (1997 and 2001), Kaplan (2004), Pusser and Turner (2004), Ramo
(1998), Richardson (1999), Tierney (2004), and the questions posed at the end
of the AGB *Statement on Institutional Governance* (1999, 11–12). It is our judgment that the *initial* step in reconciling competing governance claims requires an
understanding of the legitimate basis for these claims.

Legitimacy Claims and Practices

The internal debate about shared governance is rooted in a set of values about
legitimate behavior in the academy. These values support a view that authority and
power need to be distributed in ways that ensure that those who have the relevant
expertise/*competence* are in decisive roles. In addition, those who are *concerned*
about the issue, those whose *cooperation* is necessary to implement it, and those
whose *cash* is needed to fund it all have legitimate claims to participate. These
four claims—competence, concerns, cooperation, and cash, the four Cs of shared
governance—are the basis on which the arguments about governance rest.

The prevailing culture of academic governance is that the faculty's voice in
matters of academic affairs should be primary. Only faculty are *competent* to determine who should be members of the faculty, what should be the content of the
curriculum, and how the curriculum should be taught. Judging the effectiveness
of decisions made in these areas should be the sole responsibility of the faculty,

and the competence and expertise needed to address them are exclusive to the faculty.

Others claim that those whose *cooperation* is necessary to *implement* any policy should be involved in its formulation. This claim is consistent with human relations approaches, which recognize that effective decision making requires a fundamental concern about effective implementation. In this case the assumption is that those who have the responsibility for implementation are competent to devise the policy or the plan.

A third major claim follows from the assumption that those who are fundamentally impacted by an issue should have a voice in its resolution. This may be dismissed by some as an outgrowth of the "democratic" governance movement of the 1960s, but it is a factor in the culture of academia. For example, students who are *concerned* about degree requirements, student evaluations of teaching, and in some cases program content claim their concerns should be reflected in the opportunity to participate in any policy formulation designed to change these matters. And the list goes on. Those concerned with animal rights, the quality of the environment, or food service claim a right to participate in the policy debate and decision-making process for their area of interest.

Perhaps most important, those whose *cash* supports the institution claim a right to participate in decisions as to how the university will operate. The claims of trustees/regents, state governments, students, and others are usually buttressed by references to the financial support they provide or are responsible for distributing. The public, so the argument goes, should have a voice in how its money is spent.

Balancing and integrating the legitimacy claims of each party are major indicators of effective governance. The culture of academe requires that anyone proposing to limit involvement in governance is required to justify that limitation. This presents a challenge when setting institutional priorities. Which priorities should prevail when there is little agreement among the claimants about whose claim takes precedence? What does shared governance really mean?

There are substantial disagreements about what shared governance means (CHEPA 2003). For some it is fully collaborative decision making or the collegial model of governance. Some believe it is consultative decision making, which revolves around information sharing and discussion rather than joint decision. For others, shared governance is a set of understandings—faculty make decisions in certain areas and the administration and the board act in others. Mortimer and McConnell (1978) identified these approaches as either joint decision making or the separation of jurisdictions.

This lack of agreement on what shared governance means makes it difficult to achieve the high levels of trust and respect needed for effective governance because the parties bring to the table different expectations about their authority to determine a decision. The strategic planning case discussed in Chapter 6 illustrates how an otherwise inclusive planning process can falter if the faculty and administration have different expectations about who *acts on a plan*. The lack of trust among governance parties surfaces in many subtle ways. For example, one senses that there may be more than good-natured humor involved in the chiding that faculty leaders who move into administrative positions receive for "going over to the dark side."

On the faculty side of the matter, apathy and lack of respect for the governance process may be among the most significant barriers to meaningful faculty participation. In our view, patterns of participation in the political life of the campus reflect those in the general polity. That is, there are likely to be three groups: a small group who participate actively and serve on committees; a somewhat larger group who attempt to be aware of and knowledgeable about governance issues and may get involved from time to time; and the largest group who choose, for whatever reason, not to participate actively in governance.

It is also useful to note that shared governance mechanisms at the system and campus levels are likely to be perceived by the faculty as less effective or legitimate than those at the department or college level. And this, despite the finding of researchers that academic vice presidents perceive faculty to have more influence across various domains of decision making than faculty think they have (CHEPA 2003, 8).

Politics Trumps Shared Governance

The consequence of our observations about the practice of shared governance is that political values/principles will trump those of shared authority when big or important issues are at stake. Although defining a "big" issue is an art form, there are obvious examples, such as program closure, approaches to collective bargaining, the sanctity of tenure, and budget cuts. These issues are complicated further by the multiple areas of political action that occur both within and external to the academy. Pusser and Ordorika (2001, 149) assert that it has long been the case that "public universities and their governing boards are political institutions [and] public postsecondary policymaking is political action." Baldridge et al. (1977, 23) make the case that universities are not "standard bureaucracies." Cohen and March (1974, 2) describe them as "organized anarchies," and Birnbaum (1988, 154) refers to universities as "anarchical systems." We draw on the work of these scholars and on Julius, Baldridge, and Pfeffer's (1999) characterization of the decision-making process in asserting that four major characteristics of political systems are useful in understanding academic governance:

- Conflict is normal;
- Goals are ambiguous and contested;
- Participation is fluid; and
- Decisions are rarely final—instead, they flow; that is, they are always subject to review and revision over time.

The *implementation* of big-issue decisions—where conflict is normal, goals are ambiguous and contested, and participation is fluid—is at the heart of academic governance. Dealing with these political realities is the litmus test of effective governance and changes the bases of several of the claims that legitimate shared authority in the first place.

Political processes and values legitimate the *rules of advocacy* as a conflict resolution mechanism. Advocacy is the act of pleading for, supporting, recommending, or defending a cause. Lawyers are professional advocates, and good lawyers are first-rate advocates. Their objective is not the discovery of some ultimate truth, but rather a presentation designed to persuade their audience of an opinion in their client's favor. Generally when the advocacy process takes over, the search for truth and the time of discovery and inquiry are over. Advocates do not have a license to be dishonest or to lie, but rather, based on admissible evidence, their objective is to persuade the audience of the merits of their case (Evans 2004, 6–7).

In a higher education setting, a resort to advocacy means that defense of specific interests rises to an art form and articulation of the whole institution's interest (even the public interest) becomes problematic. Here the separate responsibilities/perspectives of three sets of actors—the administration, the faculty, and the board—come into significant conflict.

Administrators are caught in the demand for institutional efficiency and accountability, which results from the conflict between the external influences on the university and its internal traditions. They are advised by consultants and other experts on governance to concentrate the attention of boards and other institutional stakeholders on the big issues, those of strategic importance to implementing the university's mission. Yet *implementing* strategic objectives receives insufficient attention when considering whether such objectives are realistic. For example, strategic plans seldom are linked with the financial requirements to implement them. The dilemma for the administration is the same as that pointed out by Pfeffer (1992, 18–23): nothing happens once a decision is made unless someone is prepared to implement it. Making the decision is only one stage of the process.

We do not suggest that making decisions is easy and without many of the same challenges encountered in the implementation process. Deciding what position or action to bring before institutional authorities, be they boards, academic senates, presidents, or others, also requires leaders to be mission-centered, market-smart, and politically savvy.

The focus of this book, however, is primarily on how to implement decisions originating with the administration. These could be decisions over which the administration has final authority or administrative decisions/proposals that require formal board action. In this context, securing board action is part of the implementation process. In our administrative experience, *knowing what to do* (either outright or as a proposal to the board) was not nearly as difficult as *getting it done*. The case studies we use throughout highlight this reality. For example, in the tuition case, it was not difficult to know that, given the institution's low tuition base, its financial condition, and the reasonable increases proposed, a continued pattern of modest tuition increases was the appropriate decision. The difficulty was getting this decision carried out. The lesson learned time and time again was that implementing a decision—*getting something done*—is much more difficult and time consuming than figuring out what to do in the first place.

Faculty traditionally are charged with primary responsibility for educational policy and dealing with issues of curriculum, research, and faculty status. These areas are regarded as the faculty's particular domain of expertise. When big issues are on the table, competency and expertise become secondary to the conflicting goals of competing interest groups. For example, the school closure case discussed in Chapter 3 illustrates that faculty most affected by the prospect of such an action fiercely oppose it. They attack it as an unwise decision in view of community/national needs. They may even mobilize students, alumni, and community stakeholders in an effort to forestall such a closure. In political systems, such a resort to external stakeholders is legitimate.

Most public boards are typically chosen through a political process, usually by gubernatorial appointment and senate confirmation, but sometimes by popular election. Their role is deceptively straightforward: to provide oversight of the institution, to represent the public interest in the institution, and to mediate external influences on institutional behavior (Duryea 2000). There are significant sources available to help identify the characteristics of effective boards (Ingram 1997; Chait, Holland, and Taylor 1996; Kezar, Tierney, and Minor 2004a).

On the big issues, as the tuition case illustrated, boards are under enormous pressure to deviate from their standard decision-making processes, which typically find them engaging in deliberations and endorsing the recommendations of the administration. The pressures brought to bear on governing boards faced with divisive issues influence how effective they can be on such matters. Most trustees are not accustomed to the controversy surrounding big issues and are uncomfortable with public hearings where tempers flare and picket lines have to be crossed. They find it difficult to respond to hunger strikes and deal with negative press and criticism from friends and public figures. The challenge for trustees is to reach consensus on difficult issues that affect the educational mission while responding to the needs of diverse constituents and institutional stakeholders. The university is an inherent site of political struggles, and governing boards are usually the final authority for resolving big issues.

Boards operate best when there is consensus about issues brought to them. When they are asked to make controversial choices, the politics of influence as expressed through the rules of advocacy become more important. The fluidity of participation results in greater volatility than usual. Contradictory views and information are introduced, and such conflict can result in questions by trustees about whether they have the "right" information or whether the data are biased. In addition, because most public boards have to operate "in the sunshine" and are prohibited from having private conversations about board matters, the opportunities to examine alternatives and seek consensus within the board are limited. Sunshine laws represent a significant element in the functioning of public universities and are a "still-evolving public policy experiment [with a] potentially profound influence" (Hearn and McLendon 2005,

31). We are inclined to agree with the assessment of Duderstadt and Womack (2003, 157) that sunshine laws seriously constrain the operation of public university boards. These authors note that the only public organizations typically exempted from such laws are the legislative bodies that draft and the judicial bodies that extend them.

We will discuss a specific context for administrative, faculty, and board interactions in Chapter 3. Before doing so, it is appropriate to discuss the workings of two important structures through which faculty participate in campus governance: senates and unions.

SENATES

Functions of Senates

Birnbaum's treatment of the manifest and latent functions of senates in campus governance is classic and provides the basis for the following discussion. In considering why both faculty leaders and administrators continue to support the existence of senates, he argues that "it is obvious that faculty would wish to maintain senates because they are a symbol of administrative acceptance of the idea of faculty participation in governance. Administrators may support senates because voluntary faculty participation in such bodies is a tacit acknowledgment by the faculty that they recognize and accept the ultimate legal authority of the administration and the board" (Birnbaum 1989, 235).

As a symbolic body, the senate has several latent functions. It has symbolic value as a visible manifestation of faculty influence or power, and it provides some status. It recognizes one of the fundamental facts of governance—that faculty members are insistent on their right to participate in governance. Cohen and March (1974, 121) argue that, although faculty insist on their right to participate, they are less interested in exercising that right.

Birnbaum notes that in some situations the senate provides the opportunity to refer issues to it with the expectation that these issues will take up considerable energy and not be heard of again. Even in such cases, there can be an important outcome. Debate can lead to a realization that an issue thought to be fairly simple and have widespread support is in fact complex and contentious. "As the attractiveness of simplistic solutions is reduced, aspirations are modified and potential conflict is therefore managed" (Birnbaum 1989, 237).

Several other latent functions of senates are important to this discussion. Sometimes they serve as an attention cue for an issue of importance because extended discussion may signal that the matter is of unusual significance and worthy of an investment of a scarce resource—administrative time. Senates can also function as important personnel screening devices. By effective performance on senate committees, faculty members signal their availability for increasingly responsible assignments. Finally, senates play a role in campus culture. They are a place where friends can meet, engage in political intrigues, gossip about issues, pick nits, and explore in depth "the intricacies of Robert's Rules of Order" (Birnbaum 1989, 237–240).

Effectiveness of Senates

How effective are senates? Birnbaum suggests that the evidence is troublesome.

> Depending upon the organizational assumptions used, an observer might consider the senate to be effective in governance either (a) to the extent that it efficiently considered institutional problems and, through rational processes, developed rules, regulations, and procedures that resolved them, or (b) to the extent that, perceived as fully representative of its constituencies, it formulated and clarified goals and policies, or (c) to the extent that, through interaction in the senate forum, it developed shared values leading to consensus. But senates often appear to do none of these things well. From the bureaucratic perspective they are slow and inefficient, from a political position they are oligarchical and not representative, and from a collegial viewpoint faculty interactions may be as likely to expose latent conflicts as to increase feelings of community. (Birnbaum 1989, 234)

The list of criticisms and studies of the effectiveness of senates is long and quite detailed. Survey and research data show there is widespread faculty dissatisfaction with senates. Large portions of the faculty do not perceive senates to be important governance bodies. Coupled with this faculty dissatisfaction and cynicism about senates is the reality that administrators tend to attribute more influence to senates than do the general faculty (CHEPA 2003; Kaplan 2004; Minor 2003 and 2004; Mortimer and McConnell 1978; Ramo 1998).

Senates are deliberative rather than action-oriented. One often-repeated criticism is that the quickest way to delay an issue is to ask the senate for its advice. Those who favor a bureaucratic model of organization are strong on the inefficiency arguments.

In many cases, it is perceived that senates do not deal with issues that are important. There are other venues of participation that are perceived to be more influential than senates. For example, in cases where there is a practice of appointing ad hoc or special committees to deal with important academic issues, the perception of the senate as influential is weakened. Keller (1983, 61) refers to such a body as a "Joint Big Decision Committee." This type of committee is an important issue in the Mythical State case discussed in Chapter 5.

There are basic concerns about whether senates are representative of the people they are chosen to represent. As noted earlier in this chapter, widespread faculty participation in senate activities is not the norm. This lack of participation can mean that senates are perceived to lack legitimacy and effectiveness.

In a few cases administrators are excluded from participation in faculty senates. Many faculty members complain that when administrators participate in senates, they can have a "chilling" effect on the openness of debate and deliberations. Ramo (1998, 46) argues this when he states that administrators "double dip" when they participate in senate deliberations because they retain the right to veto decisions that result from these debates. Administrators claim that the failure to reflect their views in senate actions violates one of the basic claims for legitimacy in governance, namely, that those whose cooperation is necessary to implement a policy should be involved in its formulation.

The manner in which senates do business can be troublesome. A senate that moves from the occasional passage of a strong resolution to the practice of participating in governance "by resolution" risks discrediting its legitimate role. Too often such resolutions reflect ill-informed positions on complex matters. More important, they sidestep engagement with the administration in the very sort of deliberative processes that are valued in the academy and essential for shared governance. On the other hand, administrators who ask for senate consultation on a big issue at the end of the spring term or take action on a big issue without senate consultation are equally at fault for violating basic tenets of shared governance.

How the arguments for "pure" faculty senates are resolved is crucial as a campus sorts out claims for legitimate participation and establishes its eventual form of governance. The *pure* faculty voice and the *double dip* arguments do not recognize other legitimate claims—for example, those of the implementers for a place at the table before an outcome is finalized.

There are some who feel that senates in multicampus systems are kept busy implementing systemwide directives rather than dealing with issues that are important to the campuses. Also, within systems, faculty from smaller campuses may fear the influence of the flagship campus in dictating issues to be addressed or in prescribing the structure of campus senates. Smaller campuses in multicampus systems are concerned that "one size fits all" policies or solutions may not reflect the culture of their institutions.

Finally, in cases where the faculty are unionized, a determination has to be made as to whether a senate will continue to operate and, if so, how the senate and the union will separate their jurisdictions. In the literature on unionization, there is some criticism that senates constitute company unions. Senates are supported by the administration in terms of staffing and basic operations, and, when administrators have senate representation or control some senate processes, the senate cannot adequately reflect the diversity of views among the faculty.

Those institutions that are interested in determining how they can measure the effectiveness of their campus senates will find considerable help from the faculty associations. Participants at the annual meetings of the American Association of Higher Education's National Network of Faculty Senates developed and refined over a 12-year period 18 traits of effective senates (AAUP n.d.b). The AAUP, drawing on the work of Ramo (1998), makes available a set of questions for the general evaluation of shared governance, including key indicators for the governance climate, institutional communication, the roles of the board, president, and faculty, joint decision making, and structural governance arrangements (AAUP n.d.a).

UNIONS

Faculty unions have been an important part of the governance milieu in American higher education for more than 35 years. At least 32 states have extended collective bargaining rights to faculty in public institutions. In the early 1970s, changes in the interpretation of the National Labor Relations Act (NLRA) resulted in extending the right to form unions to independent institutions. Subsequent decisions by the National Labor Relations Board (NLRB) reversed this action. More recent NLRB decisions leave open some possibility for faculty unions at private institutions. Interested readers will want to review treatments of this matter by Ehrenberg et al. (2004) and Leatherman (2000). The following discussion of the growth of unions and the assumptions and issues that a collective bargaining environment presents provides the context for a series of observations about the interaction of unions with campus senates and their role in campus governance.

Growth of Collective Bargaining

The most recent compendium of data published by the National Center for Collective Bargaining in Higher Education (Hurd, Bloom, and Johnson 1998, v-xii) and data compiled by the National Center for Education Statistics (USDOE 2001, 4–10) provide basic information about faculty unions. Some 516 bargaining agents represent more than 256,000 faculty on 1,125 campuses. More than 25 percent of degree-granting postsecondary institutions have unions that represent at least some of their faculty, and 26 percent of full-time faculty are represented by unions. In the public sector about 38 percent of full-time faculty are covered by unions. Several points about the growth of faculty unions are important.

- Faculty unions are largely a creature of public higher education. Nearly 96 percent of unionized faculty are in the public sector, and approximately 92 percent of campuses with unions are public with an even division between public four-year and two-year institutions.

- Full-time faculty are more likely to have union representation than part-time faculty, and larger shares of faculty at public two-year institutions are represented by a union than those at other types of institutions.

- Nearly 90 percent of unionized faculty are concentrated in 10 large states, with nearly half found in California and New York.

- More than 100 institutions have had collective bargaining elections where the decision has been not to unionize.

Assumptions about Legitimacy

The assumptions underlying a move to collective bargaining indicate that it is a formal recognition of a political approach to shared governance. It tends to be an overt recognition that conflict is normal, goals are contested, and decisions are not made—they flow. The basic assumptions of collective bargaining illustrate this point.

The fundamental assumption of collective bargaining is that there is a conflict of interest between the employer and the employee—the board/administration and the faculty—over terms and conditions of employment. This assumption does not *require* that these differences be negotiated in an adversarial environment, although some believe this is an inevitable consequence of the model. Unions continue to argue, as pointed out earlier, that collective bargaining can be conducted in a cooperative and collegial atmosphere. Others have said that the separation of jurisdictions, like those involved in a conflict of interest situation, requires that the parties negotiate as though it is legitimate to articulate separate and different interests. Under this model, information becomes an important resource in a political equation and is used for political purposes.

A second assumption and one of the most important characteristics of unionization is the requirement that management bargain in good faith and sign a legally binding document. The legal basis for the principles of shared governance found in faculty handbooks and other institutional documents is usually state statutes or the rules and regulations of a governing board. In some instances, such policy documents can be changed without prior notification of faculty, and in other instances changes are made after consultation with faculty but on the insistence of the governing authority. Under collective bargaining, however, many of the issues addressed by such rules and regulations are considered terms and conditions of employment and have to be included in a legally binding document that cannot be changed without the agreement of both parties. Unions point out that delegated governance arrangements or powers can be reassumed and that there is no guarantee of protection against arbitrary and capricious acts. Administrators and trustees argue that theirs is the ultimate responsibility for the overall health of the institution and this responsibility cannot be ceded to other groups.

The third major assumption of unions is that of exclusivity—the requirement that management can deal only with the union and not directly with individual employees on the terms and conditions of their employment. It is clear that, under most prevailing statutes, the union has exclusive authority over terms and conditions of employment, however that is defined. Further, all faculty who are defined to be in the bargaining unit are bound by the conditions of the contract, and administrators can be held accountable for its effective implementation.

Finally, collective bargaining statutes usually provide binding dispute resolution mechanisms to deal with apparently irreconcilable disagreements between the parties. The most common examples are mediation and arbitration. Although the details of arbitration are negotiable, it can result in decisions that are binding on both parties over matters within the scope of the contract. In some cases, the strike is both permitted and practiced and becomes an important dispute resolution mechanism. Annunziato (1994) reported that over a period of nearly 30 years (1966–1994) there were 163 faculty strikes.

Observations about Unionization

A comprehensive treatment of faculty unions is not our purpose in this book. However, the legal environment under which collective bargaining occurs; the process of determining who is eligible to vote in any election and covered by the resulting contract; the dynamics of collective bargaining elections, negotiations, and contract administration; and the arbitration experience are all important in the general pattern of campus governance.

For example, the definition of who can vote in an election and who will be covered by any subsequent contract is changing and is adding a significant group of participants to the governance process, including lecturers and part-time faculty. And the definition of a bargaining unit requires a judgment about which of the teaching/professional staff share a community of interest such that they should be included in *one* unit. State statutes can vary on the way in which this unit determination is made. In one instance, a statute passed in the state of Washington specifies that there can be only one faculty bargaining unit per institution. This has been interpreted by the Public Employee Relations Commission to mean that faculty members who teach at least one-sixth of a normal load should be included in the same bargaining unit as full-time tenure track and tenured faculty. The result at Western Washington University was that 454 tenured and tenure-track faculty and 321 limited-term faculty (155 taught less than half time) were eligible to vote. The final vote was 300 for unionization and 284 against.

A related development is that graduate students are forming their own bargaining units. As of 2002–2003, more than 30 research and doctoral institutions had collective bargaining agreements covering teaching assistants (Ehrenberg et al. 2004, 222–231; Julius and Gumport 2002; Rhoades and Rhoads 2002). These two recent developments threaten to change the scope of legitimate participants in campus governance. The traditional debate about who is *qualified* to participate in shared governance is increasingly being decided by forces external to the institution—state statutes and labor relations boards.

Knowing what is *going on* in government circles is critical to the governance process of any public university. Union leaders at the state, system, and local levels often have better political "intelligence" than campus administrators and faculty. In general, system-level unions and administrators have better access to state governmental leaders (e.g., governors and legislators) than do campus administrators and faculty. System-level unions are more likely to participate in partisan political activity in favor of the candidates that support their views of state politics. Campus leaders who lack comparable access to the political dynamics of state government are at a disadvantage and as a result may lack credibility when dealing with big issues such as multiyear budget cycles.

Research, commentary, and experience lead one to assert that the dynamics of campus power and influence are modified substantially under the conditions of collective bargaining (Maitland and Rhoades 2001; Rhoades 1998). The reader will have to determine whether these modifications enhance or diminish shared governance.

SENATES AND UNIONS

What are the dynamics of campus governance when senates and unions coexist? According to Ehrenberg et al., very little is known about how unions influence faculty governance. On the matter of graduate student unions, Ehrenberg and colleagues reference concerns expressed by James Duderstadt, former president of the University of Michigan: "In addition to worrying about graduate student unions getting involved with issues of class size and the assignment of teaching assistants, he worries that graduate student unions may lead to some breakdown in the faculty-student mentorship relationship and ultimately a reduction in graduate program quality." Whether these concerns reflect reality remains to be tested (Ehrenberg et al. 2004, 230–231).

There are strong and varied views about whether senates and unions are complementary or competitive. For example, some presidents and boards illustrate this diversity of opinion by attempting to persuade faculty not to vote for unions in pending elections. One university president concluded that "a strong system of shared governance is the best method of achieving and maintaining the faculty rights and privileges which are so important in bringing about an environment which nourishes academic quality in teaching, research, and public service. Further, I believe faculty bargaining units are inimical to the growth of shared governance" (Smallwood 2004, A10). This view—that collective bargaining is not consistent with strong systems of shared governance—has been repeated in several elections where there have been attempts to persuade the faculty to vote for no representation.

On the other side of the argument, a joint statement from the higher education arms of the American Federation of Teachers and the National Education Association (AFT and NEA 2004, 6) argues that the fact of unions and collective bargaining does not and should not replace effective shared governance. These organizations take the position that unions complement rather than compete with other forms of shared governance; "the assertion that unions undermine shared governance is completely false." The AFT (2002, 9) statement on collective bargaining takes a similar view—shared governance can be complemented by the existence of faculty unions and they should not be competitive.

There are significant instances where the relationships in collective bargaining are adversarial. However, a national survey carried out by CHEPA (2003, 11) found that "institutions with collective bargaining did not report significant differences with regard to the importance placed on shared governance" in comparison with institutions without unions. So, although research indicates that shared governance in about half of all public four-year colleges and universities can be characterized as having some conflict and, to a far lesser extent, is adversarial (Kaplan 2004, 176), clearly such conflict cannot be laid solely at the feet of the collective bargaining movement.

In our consulting, research, and administrative experiences, we have come to believe that the eventual pattern of governance relations in institutions with both unions and senates depends on the culture and context of each institution. We think that resolution of the basic question—how do senates and unions coexist?—needs to take the following into account.

First, it is not known how influential senates were before collective bargaining at a given institution. In cases where unionization is the response to statewide politics, such as in New York, California, Pennsylvania, and Hawai'i, this question probably cannot be answered empirically.

Second, there is likely to be substantial overlap in the faculty leadership of a union and senate. It is not uncommon for members of the faculty bargaining team to also serve as members of the senate executive committee. About 90 percent of all institutions with unionized faculty permit faculty leaders in the bargaining unit to also serve on campus faculty governance bodies (Kaplan 2004, 189). As is the case for government in general, patterns of leadership among faculty seem to reflect the axiom that there is a limited amount of *governance energy*. Overlapping faculty leadership makes it difficult for campus administrators to maintain clear delineations between issues to be resolved with the union and those to be resolved with the senate. This conflict is a complication in the Mythical State case discussed in Chapter 5. Clearly, senate activity on mandatory bargaining issues such as salary and conditions of employment has to cease.

Third, if unionization is accompanied by a high degree of intrafaculty conflict, senates will have difficulty achieving the levels of collegiality and consensus needed to be effective. And if administrative relations with the union are adversarial, they tend to impact the tone of relations with the senate. In either situation, trust and legitimacy are low and the institution's capacity for effective shared governance is diminished.

Fourth, the broader the bargaining unit, the more likely it is that senate influence is weak. On the other hand, if the senate does not represent stakeholders who are members of the faculty bargaining unit—such as part-time faculty, lecturers, and other academic personnel—its legitimate claim to represent the campus is weakened.

There exist in higher education several different ways to reconcile the apparent differences between the jurisdictions of senates and unions when they coexist. One approach is for the union to include senate bylaws and the scope of senate responsibilities in the union contract. Under such circumstances, the senate clearly becomes a creature of the formal union documents, and changes in its scope cannot be made unless they are negotiated. Another common approach is an agreement between the senate and the union about their separate jurisdictions. Table 2.1 is an example of such an agreement.

In this agreement there is clear consensus that salaries and fringe benefits and the governance of faculty complaints are the exclusive responsibility of the union; curricular matters and educational programs are the exclusive responsibility of the senate; and the senate and union have joint responsibilities for promotion and tenure, academic standards, and other areas. We are aware of cases where the union controls governance matters more closely than this agreement suggests.

Table 2.1
Model Agreement: Roles of a Faculty Senate and a Union

Activities	Faculty Senate Role	Union Role
1. Representation of faculty	• Represent the faculty in the development of educational programs, and • Professional activities not covered by collective bargaining or law	• Represent the faculty in matters relating to the conditions of employment
2. Tenure and promotion (T&P)	• Review criteria for promotion and tenure drafted by academic departments or other institutional organizations	• All tenure and promotion procedures and format • Review T&P criteria
3. Curricula, courses, graduation requirements, and similar academic matters	• The responsibility of the senate	
4. Salaries and fringe benefits		• The responsibility of the union
5. Student relations	• All student/faculty matters unless related to a contract provision are the responsibility of the senate	• Those student/faculty problems that involve faculty status or activities specified in the union contract
6. Budget	• Consultation role exercised jointly with the union	• Consultation role exercised jointly with the senate

7. Academic standards	• Development of standards for:
	   – Professional ethics
	   – Student admission requirements
	   – Systems of student grading
		• Application of standards to individual members of the faculty

8. Grievances and faculty complaints	• Work with union on procedures for those complaints outside of the union's exclusive responsibility.	• Exclusive responsibility for all complaints and grievances dealing with:
		   – Wages
		   – Hours and conditions of employment

9. Other	• Meet with union to determine jurisdiction	• Meet with senate to determine jurisdiction

Source: Based on a "Memorandum of Agreement Regarding Roles of the University of Hawai'i Professional Assembly and the UH Faculty Senates," February 23, 1976, photocopy.

For example, in a few cases membership in the senate and its committees is limited to members of the union. In still other cases we have observed that senates atrophy and the entire set of responsibilities typically associated with faculty governance has been assumed by the union. In some of these situations we have witnessed the reemergence of senates after a hiatus of 15 to 20 years and usually after union-administrative relationship patterns have stabilized. These kinds of experiences lead us to say "it all depends" when discussions about union-senate relations arise.

SUMMARY

This chapter reviewed the cultural traditions of shared authority as the ideal or dominant governance type in the academy. We showed that there are fundamental disagreements about what shared governance actually means and how it should be practiced. We argue that, on the big issues, politics trumps shared governance and the rules of advocacy prevail.

The case is made that within the academy there is a set of values about legitimate behavior—claims to participate in governance—that need to be recognized. We call these claims the four Cs of governance—competence, concern, cooperation, and cash.

The practice of shared governance at the campus level is illustrated by a discussion of senates and unions. These campus-level governance structures reveal the complexities in shared governance as it actually operates.

In Chapter 3, we continue this discussion of shared governance by focusing on boards of trustees/regents and how they operate. We return to the case methodology used in Chapter 1 to illustrate the complexities of shared governance when boards, administrators, and faculty interact on a big issue—the closure of a professional school.

CHAPTER

The Board: Where Does It Fit in the Art of Academic Governance?

It is as important not to overguard as it is to guard well.
—Kerr and Gade, *The Guardians*

The greatest gap in perceptions of the legitimacy of shared governance within colleges and universities is between faculty and trustees. The relationship has been characterized as rocky (Tierney 2005). Faculty tend to believe that trustees have a limited role, if any, in academic affairs. In the areas of academic personnel and programs, faculty believe that their competence and need to determine and approve decisions should be paramount. In matters of what should be taught and who should teach it, faculty expect final control. The joint AAUP, ACE, and AGB statement established that in such matters faculty need to have primary authority, which should be overruled only in rare and compelling instances and for reasons communicated to the faculty (AAUP 2001, 221).

An essential element of this primacy is the belief that individual faculty members require a high degree of professional autonomy to do their work. "Academic professionals not only need to be free to explore ideas that may be strange or unpopular, but they also must be able to organize their research or to structure their daily work according to their best judgment" (Morrill 2002, 3). This belief in individual autonomy also defines the profession *collectively*. It is the profession, not government leaders, trustees, or administrators, that sets the standards that define what is acceptable and unacceptable performance or what constitutes quality and what does not.

Trustees, on the other hand, may find such beliefs difficult to understand. Their debates and concerns often center on what they perceive to be a lack of accountability or even freedom from responsibility. Many trustees see the evidence of program duplication, bloated general education requirements, and the excesses of free inquiry to be problems that require solutions. Those trustees with business experience tend to be uncomfortable with the lack of a bottom line.

Mortimer and McConnell (1978, 21–23) characterize such differences as inherent in organizations employing professionals. Such organizations experience conflict over goals and between professional and bureaucratic values. The roles of various actors in the organization come into conflict owing to different behavioral norms. A principle thesis of Rhoades's work (1998, 6) is that "academics are managed professionals" and are increasingly so because of broad and expanding managerial discretion. The struggle is one of control, and Morrill puts the dilemma quite succinctly: "As faculty members continue to experience pressure from outside and within the academy to restructure programs, respond to new types of students, cut costs, measure effectiveness, and set priorities, the conflict with the value system of academic professionals becomes intense and even hostile. In dozens of daily moments, faculty feel the full weight of institutional control. The clash in belief systems is palpable: intrinsic versus instrumental, absolute against relative" (Morrill 2002, 5).

These gaps in values and perceptions of legitimate behavior can never be fully resolved to everyone's satisfaction and, as Tierney (2005) notes, divorce is not an option. These differences must be recognized and ameliorated, however, if the art form of academic governance is to be mastered and effective. The following case of closing a school and the analysis of case dynamics appeared in an earlier work (Mortimer and Sathre 2006, 74–79 and 83–84). This case provides a specific context to illustrate how traditional governance patterns change and gaps in values and perceptions widen considerably when the academy is dealing with big issues. This chapter continues with a general discussion of boards—their structure, appointment of members, and duties and responsibilities—and makes several observations about the characteristics of effective boards.

THE SCHOOL CLOSURE CASE
Events at Glenhaven

At their last meeting of the 2000 academic year, the governing board at Glenhaven University voted to approve the administration's reorganization proposal to fold what was then a freestanding professional school into another school as a program with a narrowed scope of offerings. This action was the culmination of events traceable to accreditation concerns that had persisted for 20 years. Four years earlier (in 1996), the professional accreditation site team visited Glenhaven and observed that, except for the direness of the resource picture, the problems they identified were the same as those identified in three previous accreditation reviews. This site team's concerns culminated in the decision of the professional accrediting body to place the school on probation. After another site visit in 1999, the accrediting body informed Glenhaven officials that the probationary accreditation status of the school would be revoked one year later. The accrediting body established that revocation date so that students then enrolled could complete their degree requirements or make other arrangements.

The accrediting body's decision was based on concerns such as organizational and administrative shortcomings; the absence of a permanent dean for seven years; inadequate school resources, especially faculty; the absence of viable concentrations of programs; the lack of an active research program; and a faculty complement that lacked the breadth and depth of expertise needed to achieve the school's mission, goals, and objectives in graduate education and research. In general, Glenhaven administrators, faculty, and trustees did not dispute the findings of the accrediting body. There was little debate about the need to take corrective action and improve the quality of the school's program. But there was considerable disagreement between some Glenhaven faculty, the campus administration, and the public about the steps needed to achieve this outcome. The severity of the concerns suggested to some the need for a major overhaul of the structure and components of the program; others perceived that the solution lay in retaining and improving the existing structure.

From the campus administration's perspective, corrective action had to take place in the context of Glenhaven's eroding budget and internal and external assessments of multiple deficiencies in this school. During the previous decade, the university system had experienced major reductions to its general funding base, losing roughly 11 percent of its state support—the largest percentage loss for any state university system during that period. Given the severity of the university's fiscal situation and the reality of a dysfunctional school, the administration's preference was to discontinue the school's status as a distinct, freestanding unit and move the program into another school. By advocating this course, the administration made it clear that it was not willing to invest resources to maintain a school structure for an entity that for some time had not functioned in a manner consistent with the school's mission and goals, especially when Glenhaven's highest priority academic programs were not escaping cuts. The move would require a reduction in the scope of the program and elimination of the professional doctoral degree.

Leaders of the professional school, on the other hand, took the view that the revocation of accreditation was a direct result of the administration's actions and inaction. From this perspective, the solution was to appoint a permanent dean, restore funding to the school, exempt the school from future budget cuts, and commit to retaining an accredited school. A campus faculty senate resolution supported the maintenance of an accredited school. By the time of the 1999 accreditation revocation decision, it was also becoming increasingly clear that pursuing a merger would require the appointment of a different interim dean to help plan such a move. The administration pressed the serving interim dean for a commitment to lead this planning effort. The dean, however, responded that he did not know the parameters of the planned program and therefore could not commit to its leadership.

When the future of the school was placed on the Glenhaven governing board's July 1999 agenda, the controversies about how to best fix the situation and the future of the serving interim dean spilled over into the realm of the trustees. At the board's request, this session of the governing board became an informational briefing, and at their insistence the president announced that he would appoint a task force to provide the trustees with an independent report on the facts relating to the school and alternatives as to its future. The administration presented additional information and addressed the misperception that the university would terminate the entire program; administrators were committed to preserving generic master's programs while reducing their scope. For the remainder of the session, the board heard contradictory and often emotional testimony from approximately 20 individuals connected to the university—students, faculty, staff, and professionals in the community.

About this time, statements circulating on campus about the accrediting body's actions added to the confusion and unrest. As a result of various rumors, the Glenhaven administration contacted the accrediting body and clarified several issues. First, the revocation decision was final and, except for a possible procedural appeal, would not be reconsidered. In addition, there was no truth to the allegation that the accrediting body would no longer work with the administration and wished to work directly with the trustees. Also, public exploration of the option of accreditation as a program would not cause an instant loss of the school's current accreditation status.

After the July 1999 meeting, the president appointed an impartial task force of highly respected community leaders to evaluate the costs and benefits of maintaining a reputable, accredited school. Their specific charge was to assess state and community needs, ascertain the facts, assess national trends, evaluate alternatives to a separate school, and report to the board at its September meeting.

As the task force undertook its work, the debate about the future of the school raged on. Immense pressure was brought to bear on the administration and members of the board. A hunger strike was staged on the lawn of the main administration building; community leaders and politicians, including congressional office holders, criticized the administration and spoke in favor of the school; and the local television and print media gave the matter considerable visibility in lead stories, articles, and editorials.

In September 1999, the task force reported that it had reviewed three accreditation site visit reports; two internal university reviews of the school; financial, student, and institutional data; and a wealth of information from interested parties. The task force members also held a public meeting to give all sides an opportunity to be heard.

The major findings of the task force were these. There was a need for this program in the state, and the university should offer a quality response to this need. There was continuing demand for graduates of this program, and the school's continuing education and service efforts were effective. But the school needed to strengthen its research component. (Data showed several years when no research awards were received, and all current research awards were scheduled to end within a month. Several current training awards had a longer time frame.)

Ultimately the task force reported two options. The preferred option was to retain and rebuild the school and seek its reaccredidation. If the necessary resources were not available and deficiencies cited by the accrediting body could not be met by early summer of the next year, the task force recommended the second option: transitioning the program into another school and redefining its focus. After further discussion and emotional testimony from concerned individuals, the Glenhaven board accepted the recommendation to pursue the second option—to close the school and locate its master's program in another school. Over the course of the next year, the school remained in place as an accredited entity, a new interim dean was appointed, currently enrolled students were assisted in completing their degrees, and the administration finalized the reorganization proposal. In July 2000, one month after the final revocation of accreditation, the governing board took final action to approve the proposed merger. Currently the school no longer exists as a separate unit within the university. The professional doctorate degree is inactive, and master's programs in the field are offered through a restructured department in another school.

Case Dynamics

The closing of this school illustrates the dynamics of interactions among trustees, campus administrators, and the faculty in cases where tough or unpopular choices have to be made. When such issues are involved, traditional paths of governance are questioned, information becomes a political resource used to the advantage of the parties, and external interests are courted for their support. The decision-making process was intense, emotional, and complex, which was evidence of the lengthy history of the school as part of the institutional structure and the involvement of community members who felt a vested interest in the school. Each party held a unique conception of what the program should involve and ultimately what role Glenhaven should play in service to the community. Although a basic principle of institutional processes is related to the "inseparability of organization and environment" (Chaffee 1985, 89), such complexity adds to the difficulty of reaching collaborative decisions.

Glenhaven trustees debated whether they should support the administration, as well as whether the specific decision was a wise one. If they chose to reject the administration's recommendation, they were likely to weaken the administration's ability to make hard choices. If they supported the administration, but it was not a decision in the best interests of the state, the trustees were not fulfilling their obligation to protect the public interest and serve the public good. And finally, because the Glenhaven trustees were not experts in the subject matter at stake, whose data could they trust? In public meetings, program advocates made claims of dire results if the school closed—grants would be lost, students would go elsewhere, and the overall reputation of the university would suffer. Most of these claims were disputed by the administration, but the board wondered how the conflicting information could be reconciled. Who was telling the truth here? Considering the competing demands and opinions, which decision was best for the university and the state?

The Glenhaven administration was not willing to commit the funds necessary to sustain the school's programmatic scope under the leadership of a faculty it deemed to be less than stellar. Administrators doubted that a faculty previously focused on training rather than research could be reoriented to accomplish the research mission of a graduate professional school. The accreditation team was clear—the faculty as a whole had not met the accreditation standard in this regard. Yet Glenhaven's faculty and school leaders believed that all these problems were resource-driven and could be corrected by an infusion of funds (roughly $700 thousand to $1 million), hiring a permanent dean, and exempting the school from further cuts to the university's budget should they come. But the institution suffered from ongoing budget cuts and the loss of financial support across the university. For almost a decade, the university had suffered from a declining allocation of funds from the legislature. Funding, staffing, and research concerns all underlined the larger question: Through what means could Glenhaven most effectively fulfill its educational mission and serve the public good?

Some individual trustees were clearly under intense pressure from acquaintances on the faculty and in the professional community who supported the school. These community/faculty advocates were vocal and insistent that the loss of the professional school as a freestanding entity would be a major blow to Glenhaven, the identity and prestige of the faculty, and practicing professionals in the state. Community supporters of the school maintained that the inability to grant the professional doctorate would be damaging to the overall region; they also argued that it was the role of the institution to responsively serve the needs of the public. According to these advocates, the board should reject the administration's proposed action and force it to commit the funds to reaccredit the school. Whatever the board decided, it had to operate in "the sunshine," and individual trustees would have to vote on the matter in a public meeting with the television cameras rolling. External expectations and the traditions of shared governance clash when issues like this one are at stake.

The Glenhaven case focuses attention on the governing board's final responsibility for resolving disputes when internal consensus is not present. The question then arises as to what are the dynamics of board/trustee behavior. How can these individuals perform well under such intense pressure? We now turn to a discussion of boards and factors that affect their performance.

BOARD STRUCTURE, DEMOGRAPHICS, AND APPOINTMENTS

In American higher education there are 50,000 trustees and regents presiding over more than 4,000 institutions, of which approximately 40 percent are public and 60 percent are private/independent. Fewer than 10,000 trustees govern the public sector through statewide governing boards, system or multicampus boards, and individual campus boards (Ingram 1997, 3; USDOE 2003, 296). There is wide diversity in the structure and functions attributed to these various types of governing boards. Problems in operation are similar no matter what the structure of the board may be, but the purpose of boards and how they operate can be quite different, as we will demonstrate in the following discussion.

The methods of appointment and selection of board members vary with the type of board involved. Boards of independent institutions are typically self-perpetuating, and a major task is to recruit, orient, and retain effective board members. Independent boards typically are larger than public boards, the average being about 20 members. It is common for such boards to have an elected executive committee that meets monthly or bimonthly, whereas the full board meets only three or four times a year. Some seasoned observers of independent boards often refer to the "three Ws" of board appointment—wealth, wit, and wisdom. Independent boards consider carefully the ability of its members to actively participate in fund-raising efforts. Wit and wisdom are, of course, desirable qualities for all board members.

There are independent boards that have special relationships with religious orders or other support groups. The boards of some religion-affiliated institutions may be divided among members of the founding order and lay members. A separate lay board may be advisory or primarily involved in fund-raising. A major transition in the last 30 years has resulted in fewer religious orders or churches maintaining the kind of control over board appointments that characterized the first 70 years of the twentieth century.

A growing number of boards of independent institutions make provisions for a specific number of alumni to be elected to their board. In a few cases, such elections can be controversial when alumni interest groups grow critical of past elections or simply want different interests reflected on the board (Fain 2006a, A25–26).

The case of public boards and their appointment is quite different. Here there are a host of political issues, including how to work with governors, legislators, and other stakeholders who claim a right to participate in board affairs. In addition, the usual size of public boards is from 5 to 12 members, less than half the size of boards of independent institutions, and this presents a number of challenges. A single person can dominate or disrupt a small board. It is more difficult for a small board to have the needed skills to develop a good committee structure; the appointment or replacement of a single individual on a small board can change the direction or behavior of the board and the political situation of the president (Kerr and Gade 1989, 47–48).

There are at least five ways in which public board members are selected: appointment by the governor with confirmation by the senate; election by local or state constituents or by external special interest groups such as alumni; appointment as ex-officio members; appointment or election to represent internal constituents—either faculty or students; and, in a few cases, some board members may be chosen by the board itself.

It is often the case that a board is made up of members who are chosen by a combination of methods. For example, the University of Pittsburgh's board reflects its roots as an independent institution. Some of its members are chosen by the board and others are appointed by the governor. The board of Pennsylvania State University has 32 members, including five ex-officio and 21 chosen by elections or appointed by a variety of groups or authorities such as legislative leaders, alumni, faculty, and community agricultural and industrial societies. Six members are appointed by the governor (Kerr and Gade 1989, 202–203).

Hermalin describes the composition, number, and meeting frequency of boards at four distinguished universities (California, Michigan, Harvard, and Princeton). He finds that, despite great variation in (1) selection methods (appointed by governors, trustees, or other constituencies; elected by the public, alumni, or trustees; or self-perpetuating); (2) board composition (trustees/regents, alumni, students, presidents, governors, and other state officials); (3) number of trustees (9 to 40); and (4) the frequency of meetings (5 to 15 times annually), "the structure of its board of trustees has no effect on a university or college's performance" (Hermalin, 2004, 34). It is obvious that many different board structures can be successful. In our experience, what is important is whether board bylaws are clear about the role of the board, that members act in accordance with their role, and, when they don't, that the board has the capacity to police itself.

Gubernatorial Appointment and Senate Confirmation

By far the most common method of choosing trustees in the public university sector is gubernatorial appointment with senate confirmation. Several issues are associated with this method. For example, the governor of a large state may have to make more than 3,000 appointments to various boards, commissions, and committees. The dynamics involved in sorting and sifting applicants and nominees and dealing with commission, board, and committee supporters is a bureaucratic task of the highest order. The specific dynamics in a given state are much dependent on the state's political and cultural environment. A newly elected governor can be pressured by supporters who were influential in his/her success to appoint them to the prestigious university boards.

There is strong pressure to put political supporters on prestigious boards as either a reward for their past loyalty or in anticipation of their future support. In most cases these appointments reflect the appointee's ability to serve as a trustee. Some state statutes require, as was the case for Glenhaven, that appointees be from specific jurisdictions or geographic areas of the state or that they represent specific constituencies.

Appointments to the less prestigious academic boards often require a diligent search for competent, able people who are willing to serve. The political equation of power, politics, and prestige suffers when the last P, prestige, is removed. The search for appointees to less prestigious boards can be a significant problem. In some states, the culture is such that people are persuaded to serve on these boards as a "training ground" or as a civic responsibility. Some of those who serve on less prestigious boards improve their chances of being appointed to the more prestigious boards at a later time.

An illuminating story occurred during a series of interviews with a university president in a large eastern state. At the end of a governor's eight years in office, he reminisced with the president of one of his state's major public universities. The president couldn't resist asking the governor why he had appointed trustee Jones to the university's board. The president told the governor that this individual was the worst trustee with whom he had to deal in his decade of service to the university. The governor was surprised at such an evaluation and immediately got on the phone to his staff in the state capitol. The staff replied, "Governor, on that one we made a mistake." It turned out that the governor thought he was appointing a prestigious labor lawyer from the western part of the state by the name of Jones. The person he actually appointed was a travel agent named Jones from a small rural town. Apparently the staff had confused the two. Trustee Jones served a full term on the board and the president made the evaluation that he was the worst, "most intrusive" trustee that he had to deal with. The point of the story is that mistakes are made in the board appointment process, even at a major university, and are even more likely at the less prestigious institutions.

The Association of Governing Boards of Colleges and Universities has been critical of a board appointment process that rewards the political friends of a newly elected governor with little attention to their qualifications to serve. Political connections alone are not sufficient criteria when considering the leadership qualifications for an academic enterprise. AGB supports a screening process whereby candidates for service on boards get nominated and undergo screening from either an existing blue ribbon committee or a committee designed specifically for this purpose. At least five states (Kentucky, Massachusetts, Minnesota, North Dakota, and Virginia) have a screening mechanism to identify qualified candidates for some board appointments. Under such a system, prospective applicants or nominees undergo a vetting process and their qualifications are reviewed. The legislature or governor is then provided with a slate of candidates from which to choose nominees or make appointments (AGB 2003; Massachusetts Board n.d.). Assuming that screening committee membership is not limited to specific constituencies, this process has the potential to improve the chances that qualified appointments will be made and gives a governor some "cover" from the pressure to appoint political friends. Interested readers will find helpful the selection criteria outlined by the CHEPA scholars (Kezar, Tierney, and Minor 2004b) for evaluating individual board nominees and the composition of the board as a whole.

Elected Boards

In at least four states (Colorado, Michigan, Nebraska, and Nevada) some regents/governing board members are chosen in statewide elections. This is true for the three constitutional universities in Michigan. In Colorado, Nebraska, and Nevada there are statewide elections. In 17 states community college boards are chosen in local school board elections or elections held specifically for the purpose of trustee selection (Hebel 2004).

The election of trustees raises the question of the extent to which partisan politics should be a factor in selecting trustees. In at least a few cases, the decision to run for a trustee position in statewide elections is the first step in a hoped-for political career. In many cases, running in these elections requires the candidate to raise money; solicit endorsements from unions, manufacturing groups, and other interested stakeholders; and carry out the other activities of political campaigns.

In local school board and community college elections, the realities of partisan politics tend to be magnified. There is the danger that conflicts of interest can affect a trustee chosen in a local election. When teacher union endorsements become a key ingredient in one's ability to get elected, the question arises as to whether the candidate so endorsed can participate effectively as a member of a management team responsible for negotiating subsequent contracts with the endorsing union. The issue here, as well as in the case of appointees who are selected to "represent" certain sections of the state or voter interests, is whether these interests can be balanced against the good of the institution as a whole.

Faculty and Student Board Members

The practice of appointing members of faculty and student stakeholder groups to boards is increasing. The central state coordinating or governing boards in at least 9 states have faculty representation and those in 39 states have student members (ECS 1997, 235–250). The rationale for such appointments is to represent important stakeholders in the board room. Again, the issue that arises is whether a faculty trustee has a conflict when the board is discussing important matters such as faculty salaries or is voting on tenure and promotion policies and appointments. Certainly, the faculty view should be articulated when considering these issues, but it is difficult to understand how a trustee who is also an active faculty member avoids having at least a marginal conflict of interest in such situations.

The same issue affects a student who is appointed to represent student interests when the matter of tuition is on the table. It would be an interesting research question to poll voting student members of governing boards when the issue of tuition is before the board. The question is, under what conditions could a student member of the board vote for an increase in tuition?

Somewhat similar issues come up when trustees are appointed by the governor or are elected to represent certain areas of the state. The challenge is whether the board serves specific interest groups or the public interest at large. The dilemma for a trustee chosen to represent such interests or a geographic area is how to perform that function adequately while considering the interests of the institution as a whole. This is one of the fundamental challenges in building a cohesive board in public institutions. In the context of this book, it is difficult to argue that a trustee's responsibility is to represent the whole institution if he/she is chosen to represent the interests of a constituent group or geographic area. In such cases the trustee is *chosen to be an advocate* for a set of interests. This perpetuates the legitimacy of advocacy as a basis for shared governance debates.

Based on three decades of work with appointed, elected, and ex-officio public board members at multiple institutions, we find agreement with the variation in behavior linked to trustee backgrounds described by James O. Freedman, former president of the University of Iowa and Dartmouth. "The board members at Iowa, drawn from a wider social spectrum and a more diverse set of occupations, tended to have a more realistic appreciation of the limits on the president's power to dominate his constituencies. The board members at Dartmouth, most of whom had substantial management experience ... tended to assume that a chief executive officer could readily impose his will upon faculty and students alike if he only wanted to" (Freedman 2004, 11).

Drawing on Freedman's observations, having student or faculty members on a board can add to the diversity of the board and potentially its overall effectiveness. In our experience, the test is whether these or other board members chosen by specific constituencies can put on the *mantle of the whole*, that is, rise above the circumstances of their appointment and adhere to standards that place the welfare of the institution above that of one specific group. We also note that the good of the whole institution can take a back seat when individuals appointed to boards, regardless of their background or experience, use their time of service as a steppingstone to advance personal career goals.

STATEWIDE AND SYSTEM BOARDS

Although they share many of the problems of institutional boards, statewide and multicampus boards deserve special mention. Many of the problems in state higher education policy leadership are rooted in who is chosen to serve on these entities.

McGuinness's (2003) typology of statewide postsecondary education structures and their corresponding responsibilities is very helpful. He identifies 23 states that have consolidated governing boards with responsibility for all public higher education in the state. Another 24 states have coordinating boards whose authority varies from state to state. Typically these boards have some program-approval functions and authority to either review and recommend or approve budgets. Three states have planning or service agencies.

The result is a collage of state postsecondary education coordination and governance models. Perhaps the best known of these is in California. Since 1960, it has had a state coordinating agency, the California Postsecondary Education Commission (CPEC), with the authority to make recommendations on policy issues confronting the governor and the legislature, and to review and recommend action on postsecondary education budgets. Despite the responsibilities lodged with CPEC, it is generally agreed that the real "power" in California resides with the governing boards of the three separate segments: the University of California, the California State University and College System, and the California Community College System.

State-level governing boards in states such as Arizona, South Dakota, and Hawai'i have absolute control over a variety of state institutions. In South Dakota, the board governs six public universities. The Arizona board of regents has governance authority over the University of Arizona, Arizona State University, and Northern Arizona University. In Hawai'i the governing board presides over a

10-campus university system consisting of a research university, two comprehensive institutions, and seven community colleges. In addition, the Hawai'i board has responsibility as the state postsecondary education commission and the state career and technical education board.

There is great variability in the way in which these boards function and the legitimacy of the issues and questions raised in the course of their operation. For example, the University of California board presides over 10 institutions classified as research universities. The University of Hawai'i board presides over a collage of institutions with different missions. The organized research mission is limited to the research university campus at Mānoa whereas the broad access/open-door function is limited to the seven community colleges. In addition, two of the community colleges (on Kaua'i and Maui) have a virtual monopoly on educational services on these islands and therefore have unique missions. In this respect the Hawai'i system is similar to other systems (e.g., City University of New York and the Pennsylvania State University) that include campuses with substantially different missions.

The action record of one system board, the Board of Higher Education in Massachusetts, is an excellent example of how an activist board leader can shape board authority and dynamics and deeply affect governance policies and practices at the campus level. The Massachusetts board has governing authority over 15 community colleges and 9 four-year comprehensive universities and coordinating authority over the five campuses of the University of Massachusetts. Bastedo reports that the appointment by the governor of an activist, politically well connected, and influential board chair resulted in the development and implementation during a five-year period (1995–2000) of "an incredible range of policies in academic affairs, student financial aid, and mission differentiation." These policies involved substantial change in admissions standards and access to remedial education, the lowering of student tuition and fees, joint admissions and seamless transfer policy, mission alignment and incentive funding, establishment of special colleges, and the installation of program productivity standards resulting in the termination of 52 programs in one year alone (Bastedo 2005, 556–557).

Whether the Massachusetts system policy changes were appropriate and will have lasting campus impact, we leave for others to judge. The message here is that, in one way or another, *individuals appointed to system boards can and do make a difference at the campus level*. The major challenge faced by those serving on system boards is to advance and balance institutional performance with educational performance in areas of broad public interest—two worthy outcomes that are not necessarily the same thing. In our experience, board decisions are too often made with limited understanding of the long-term policy ramifications for both the campus and the state. For example, boards may authorize programs that have the effect of expanding campus missions without regard to the long-term funding implications of such authorizations. At a later date, the system board is surprised when it is faulted for not providing the funds needed to support an expanded campus mission. System boards may make tuition and other financial decisions that can, over time, take campuses in the direction of privatization without regard for the populations that such actions may disadvantage. In these and many other matters, if system board members are chosen with the understanding that their job is to advocate for special interests, they may lack the incentive to understand the importance of decisions that are based on campus missions and policies and that advance the academic core of the institutions they oversee and the public policy agenda of the state.

BOARD DUTIES AND RESPONSIBILITIES

The literature on higher education contains a number of treatments designed to specify the scope of responsibilities for a governing board. Nason provided an excellent treatment of this topic in 1982. His work and that of Ingram (1997) are the major references for the summary of trustee responsibilities that follows.

The primary duty of the board is to hire, evaluate, and support the president. This may involve paying attention to such topics as "the care and feeding of a president," including salary, housing, and a variety of personal support matters. Monitoring a president's performance, if done well, can benefit the president and the board by focusing on goals and priorities, and it can also direct attention to the board's responsibility to assess its own performance. AGB has published extensively on presidential searches, the need to evaluate presidents on a regular basis, and how to live with presidents (Ingram 1997; AGB 1996). Fisher (1991) has provided a thorough analysis of presidential appointment processes, assessment, and compensation.

A second major responsibility of governing boards is to hold the assets of the institution in trust. This responsibility requires monitoring the financial health of the institution, managing endowments, advocating for adequate resources, raising money, and a host of accounting and financial matters.

The third set of related responsibilities includes setting and clarifying institutional mission and purpose, insisting on long-term planning, and providing oversight of academic matters. The board's role in program oversight and monitoring is illustrated by the school closure case. A number of recent treatments of this topic offer strong and sound advice to trustees. Morrill (2002 and 2003) concentrates on the board's responsibilities and strategic leadership in academic affairs. Massy (2003, 6–8) argues that the fundamental academic task confronting universities is to restore "education competency" to the academic enterprise. And Ewell (2006) provides boards with advice on issues surrounding their role in overseeing the academy's most important function, the education of students. He makes the case that understanding the academic condition of the enterprise is as critical for a board as knowledge about the institution's fiscal condition. Boards need patience in these matters, but they should not stop asking questions.

A fourth function of boards is to serve as a two-way bridge or buffer between the public and the institution. This requires preserving institutional independence and defense of academic freedom. It also means representing the broad public interest (not specific interest groups) in the institution. In the school closure case, the public attention given to the issue put great personal pressure on individual board members to reject the administration's recommendation and keep the school open. It also illustrated the board's role in interpreting the public good.

Closing a graduate professional school in a public research university highlighted a fifth responsibility of boards—to serve as a court of last resort in resolving internal disputes.

BOARD EFFECTIVENESS

Several generalizations about board effectiveness are offered by researchers and scholars of the topic. For example, Kerr and Gade (1989, 47–48) point out that boards are only as good as their members, and there is great variability here. They argue that the size of a board makes a difference—too small creates a problem in covering the subject matter, and large boards encourage the formation of executive committees and too many inactive or absentee trustees.

> The "typical" or "representative" board of trustees does not exist. Each board is in one way or another *sui generis*. Thus, any in-depth study of boards is an examination of idiosyncrasies. This is the reality. The danger in such an examination is that the more one knows about boards, the more confused about them one can become. The greater dangers, however, are to think and to act either (1) as though boards are all alike or (2) as though, at the other extreme, they have no important similarities at all. (Kerr and Gade 1989, 57)

Kerr and Gade (1989, 57–65) also discuss two basic dimensions of board performance: the nature and degree of board involvement in the life of the institution— what boards do, and the conduct of the internal political life of the board—how boards act as political mechanisms. The first dimension considers three degrees of participation: perfunctory, balanced, or intensive. For example, the *out-to-lunch board* follows the recommendation of the president in an automatic way, whereas at the other extreme the *managerial board* deals with detailed issues on a regular basis. Obviously, neither board is desirable.

The internal political life of the board is characterized as dominated, balanced, or fractionated. The *captive board* is dominated by outside authority—the governor, the sponsoring church, an economic interest group, a faculty or trade union, or a faction of the alumni. At the other end of the spectrum, the *individually fragmented board* has members who go on their self-chosen paths based on political views, concerns for disparate elements of the institution, or various controversial issues (Kerr and Gade 1989, 61–65). These rudimentary categories signal the broad range of issues that different types of boards are likely to attend to and, in turn, provide insight into the variability of board effectiveness.

A treatment of independent board competencies is offered by Chait and colleagues. After interviewing more than 100 board members and presidents at 22 independent liberal arts and comprehensive colleges, they found that effective (strong versus weak) boards demonstrated competencies or skills along six dimensions: contextual, educational, interpersonal, analytical, political, and strategic. And they concluded that board self-assessments are of questionable validity (Chait, Holland, and Taylor 1991, 1–3).

A more recent piece by the Center for Higher Education Policy Analysis (CHEPA) concentrates on the performance of public boards. Researchers interviewed 132 individuals, including board members, presidents, chancellors, governors and their staff, national association leaders, and faculty, students, and consultants who worked with boards. This study identified five elements of effective, high-performing boards: leadership, structure, culture and relationships, ongoing education, and external relations (Kezar, Tierney, and Minor 2004a).

The CHEPA scholars argue that effective public governing boards lead, not manage, and have the following characteristics.

- They discuss education and the heart of the educational mission and do not just vote on routine issues.
- The board leadership function includes effective board chairs and strong staff support, the creation of a common vision and purpose, and the development of broad-based, multiyear agendas.
- They control their structure—they clearly define their role, focus on their work plan, establish an evaluation structure, and plan for board succession and turnover.
- They foster relationships and communication that model and build a sense of acceptable behavior and a culture of professionalism.
- They establish strong relations between the president and the board chair, encourage communication between the president and individual board members, and engage with university constituents, including faculty, staff, and students, as appropriate.
- They engage in education and learning, including a strong orientation program for new members, ongoing professional development, and board evaluation.
- They have positive relationships with the governor; engage in joint formulation of goals among the governor, the board, and other stakeholders; and take advantage of situations where individual board members have the governor's ear. They stay on agenda even as new governors want to change paths. (Kezar, Tierney, and Minor 2004a, 3–7)

Of all the characteristics of effective boards described by the CHEPA scholars, we would elevate the importance of having bylaws that clearly specify the role of the board, with a strong emphasis on board involvement with major policy issues. This approach requires delegations of authority to the administration and can, if implemented, reduce board micromanagement and clarify who's accountable. After several public controversies, the University of Colorado System board recently moved in this direction. Among issues cited in the Colorado case was the realization that, when athletics reports to a board committee, it is difficult to know who "owns" the problems in that program (Fain 2006b).

SUMMARY

This chapter began by asserting that the greatest gaps in perceptions of the legitimacy of shared governance are between faculty and trustees. We used the school closure case to illustrate how politics trumps collegiality when big issues are at stake. This case displays the dynamics and interaction among boards, administrators, and faculty as they all respond to significant internal and external pressures. These pressures included the loss of school accreditation if action were not taken, the administration's commitment to a structural change, the faculty's belief that the administration should find the money to save the school, the various views of politicians, the recommendations of a special committee, and the board's responsibility to abide by open meeting statutes and make the final decision. The political pressures brought into play (demonstrations, hunger strikes, letters to the editor) meant the decision had great public visibility and illustrate how the politics of advocacy replace shared governance protocols when a big issue emerges.

To shed light on factors that affect the performance of boards, we discussed board structures and type, various appointment processes, changing membership, and roles and responsibilities. All of these factors and others influence the effectiveness of boards and help us understand their capacity to operate under intense pressure in politically charged environments.

In Chapter 4 we explore how board expectations about student transfer are translated into policy and can result in a governance clash when an academic program is viewed as a corporate responsibility.

CHAPTER

Governance of Programs
and the Curriculum

Sailing a ship across the Pacific is no different from organizing a college or university for performance improvement. In both instances, it is immensely helpful if we can come to some agreement on which way to aim the pointy end.

—Daniel Seymour, *Once Upon a Campus*

The previous chapter illustrated how the interactions of board, administration, and faculty can be contentious when unit closure or merger is the issue. Involvement of the parties in the routine of program development, evaluation, and governance is where much of the conflict associated with the art of governance originates.

This chapter reviews the nature of academic program development and evaluation and organizational structure as they affect governance. It shows where the potential conflicts lie when matters of legitimate control are at issue and argues that a program of study is not just a faculty responsibility, but a responsibility of the institution as a whole. This corporate responsibility requires the institution to answer questions such as:

- Why are programs constantly added to the curriculum, approval sought after the fact, and few, if any, ever deleted?
- Why can't university students graduate on time?
- Why don't credits transfer more freely between institutions?

The program authorization and graduation rate discussions are rooted in national debates about these topics and in our experience as administrators and consultants for several institutions. The transfer issue is the subject of a specific case in a multicampus institution with two- and four-year institutions, including a research university.

As in other chapters, we highlight the issue of governance, not academic content. Who has a legitimate claim to decide these issues, and where and when should they be decided?

PROGRAM DEVELOPMENT—THE EVOLUTION OF KNOWLEDGE

Unfortunately for those who favor rational systems, programs evolve rather than appear. Much of college and university activity in program development and evaluation is part of the routine of how faculties perform their mission of teaching, service, and research. We can offer typical examples in the following discussion, but individual experiences differ widely. For example, community colleges pride themselves on their ability to respond quickly to community needs, whereas the response time of universities tends to be longer.

It is common for new courses and options to appear based on developments in the discipline or field of study, faculty interests, available external support, and demonstrated community need. Knowledge creation and dissemination are, after all, the core of a university's mission. Fields of study and disciplines are constantly evolving, and courses, entire curricula, and departmental identity reflect these changes. In the natural sciences, for example, life sciences have evolved into innumerable specialties. In addition to biology, it is common to find programs of study in cell biology, molecular biology, and microbiology that exist as departments in many arts and sciences colleges and in medical schools. In agriculture, the life sciences may include entomology, plant pathology, plant and environmental biotechnology, and others. Mathematics departments have spun off statistics and computer science departments, as well as departments of applied actuarial sciences. The study of languages and literature has evolved into innumerable specialties based on geographic areas or countries and subject matter disciplines such as writing, literature, and communication.

The examples are endless, but a good illustration of this program evolution phenomenon is the study of management. Most analysts would agree that this field of study is basically rooted in the social sciences, and some suggest that it is appropriately taught only at the graduate level. It is common, however, for management to be taught at community colleges and in a variety of schools and colleges at any major university, including arts and sciences, education, physical education, business, engineering, and health. Most of these units teach their own courses on management and accompany them with their own brand of statistics.

Faculty and Student Interest

New programs often come about as the outgrowth of an independent study course designed for a small group of students or on the basis of faculty interest and expertise. Additional courses are developed and are grouped as an area of study within an existing program. Eventually, new programs are built on these groupings, often becoming specializations, options, minors, and eventually formal majors within departments. This evolution may ultimately result in new departments or status as a separate school.

The first stages of this evolutionary process are often unknown to campus administrators, some deans, and even department chairs. As faculty and student interests evolve, the discipline matures and expands and, in many instances, the governance mechanisms become important only after the fact.

Curriculum committees may exist at all levels of the institution, including the department, college, campus, and sometimes even at the multicampus system or state level. In the early stages, particularly at the department level, however, "senatorial" courtesy prevails. The existence of courses and their subject matter are treated as domains of individual faculty autonomy rather than as matters of institutional focus.

The first governance contact may be with the departmental curriculum committee and can be complicated by the fact that the course has already been offered through independent study or as an area of emphasis within a previously approved course. Great deference is paid to individual faculty in such instances, and further deference is given to departmental autonomy when the matter reaches higher levels of authority. This deference is usually justified on the basis that no additional resources are needed to accomplish the new emphasis or course. The fact that faculty time required for such courses means less faculty time available for other endeavors is rarely acknowledged. It is not uncommon for the "it takes no resources" argument to surface when entire programs are subject to campus prioritization activities (Dickeson 1999, 91–93). The result of this chain of events is that programs of study often *emerge* and are not the result of systematic planning.

External Support

Research programs often evolve in response to available external support, usually from federal or state government. For example, federal agencies decide they want to study the El Niño phenomenon and university faculty receive grants for this purpose. Either as part of the grant proposal or the evolution of the research effort, an institute for the study of El Niño is established within the university. Formal recognition of the institute by the governance structure may well come some time later when administrators recognize that they are dealing with a *fait accompli*.

Other federal agencies might want to study a specific health problem such as cancer or cystic fibrosis, and university faculty and administrators mount a joint effort to secure these funds in part based on a commitment to build institutes for cancer or cystic fibrosis. The bottom line is that most research universities carefully monitor the funding opportunities available from federal agencies and, either through individual faculty efforts or as institutional responses, slant their proposals to meet these externally based requirements. It is not unusual for administrators or faculty to bring the resulting program or organizational entity forward for formal approval well after the reality of its existence.

Demonstrated Community Need

In many cases the community may demand that a new program be developed. For example, community colleges pride themselves on their ability to respond quickly to the movement of local industry or changes in the job market. This is especially the case when nondegree or certificate programs that meet the need for in-service or professional upgrading are involved.

In other cases, states and university systems establish incentives for higher education institutions to provide research or training in priority areas that support the economic development of the state. Several states have developed incentive programs that make it attractive for universities to train more computer scientists, teachers, and nurses. In return for increased funding or other incentives, universities may agree to increase their emphasis in certain "high demand" areas that are important to the state's economic development.

PROGRAM GOVERNANCE

Program Approval Realities

The point of the preceding discussion is that programs are in constant motion. They evolve over time, and in many cases the governance system becomes involved after the fact. For example, once courses or options have been offered through either independent study or other flexible mechanisms, the formal governance system is in a position of approving the status quo rather than a new initiative. Further, the administration or the board may be confronted with ratification of an already functioning program or one with external money already committed.

When new offerings reach the administration or board for approval, issues of program content have usually been debated by faculty committees. The administration or the board can refuse to support such programs principally due to a lack of resources rather than any concern about program content. As Morrill has pointed out, the board can ask intelligent questions about such issues, but can rarely get involved in questions having to do with content.

> So, the question about the board's possible intervention in the curriculum seems to answer itself. Under most scenarios, it is a bad idea. It may even be a dangerous idea if ideological or political influences press a board to interfere in the curriculum. The board's first responsibility is always to the well-being of the institution, and efforts from special interests to control the board's conduct, especially if motivated by ideology, can undermine academic integrity. If boards or other stakeholders are convinced that the curriculum is in ideological disarray, they have a variety of ways to respond. The answer, however, is not to install its own curriculum. (Morrill 2002, 55)

The problem is, of course, that boards do not always exercise the restraint suggested by Morrill. For a variety of reasons they may become more involved in the details of the curriculum than is desirable. First, boards are often not well educated about the evolutionary nature of the curriculum; they realize that they are being asked to approve a course of study that may already be operational, and they resent what they perceive as a disregard for their authority to "approve new programs." Further, institutional policy may include resource requirements as a required component of program proposals, but by the time a new degree offering reaches the board for approval, it is often presented as requiring no (or very few) additional resources. Boards are skeptical of such claims, and their frustration may take the form of inappropriate questions about content or other program details that belong in the governance domain of faculty.

It can be particularly frustrating for system administrators or boards when presented with program actions that are outside the authorized mission of an institution. Although it may seem straightforward from a campus perspective to modify its mission (for example, from associate to baccalaureate level) in the context of a proposed new program, boards and system officers will view such changes as having far-reaching resource, staffing, and accreditation consequences. The resulting conflicts can spill over into big issues when special interest groups and government and business leaders become advocates for near-term actions that leave boards and administrators with long-term financial commitments.

The who, when, and how of new program development come into sharp relief when policies require prior approval to plan new programs. Based on our experience in one statewide higher education system over a 25-year period, a *prior approval to plan* requirement did little to focus the program approval process, address the complexities surrounding program development, or clarify the governance roles of faculty and the board. From the perspective of at least some faculty, implementing such a process in the academic community suggests that some administrative authority presumes to give faculty *prior approval to think*. Those who comply with the requirement quickly recognize that it is an opportunity to make as strong a case as possible for a new program—what was intended as a one- or two-page request to plan turns into a nearly complete program proposal, much of which may already be in place. And from the administrative perspective, there seems very little basis for ever denying an authorization to plan. Who approves what and when they approve it can become a very messy business.

Credential Closure Realities

Things don't get any easier at the closure end of the spectrum. Degree and certificate programs usually don't come to an abrupt halt; like old soldiers, they tend to fade away. Governing boards that retain the authority to close programs can be faced with authorizing closure of an offering that for all practical purposes no longer exists. Boards may make their frustration visible by asking, "Why are we asked to approve new offerings, but rarely asked to close down programs?" When presented with evidence that they do, in fact, act to terminate degree offerings, it is not uncommon for boards to discount such actions because "those programs were already dead." A positive outcome of such discussions can be the opportunity to educate boards about the evolutionary nature of curriculum development, why active and healthy programs are rarely terminated, and the corporate issues in which the board might more appropriately engage.

A Better Use of Time

We argue that the attention that some governing boards give to the approval and termination of individual program certificates and undergraduate majors at established public institutions with well-defined missions could be delegated to the administration. A better use of board time would be to focus on their corporate responsibility for mission clarity, hold institutions to program offerings that are within board-authorized missions, insist that institutions prioritize programs and present budget requests consistent with established priorities, focus on authorizing graduate programs that are consistent with campus missions and for which there is a demonstrated need and an adequate funding stream, and require performance assessments that reflect attention to state needs and changing student demographics. Ewell's (2006) treatment of the board's role in academic programs provides an excellent set of questions a board should ask while it keeps its hands out of too much detail.

In the following discussion we make the case that, in the matter of the curriculum, boards have a corporate responsibility to use their authority to place greater emphasis on what is learned versus what is taught. And the board's corporate responsibility extends to curricular requirements such as general education that are not the governance domain of any one department or even a single campus.

Corporate Responsibility

The primary issue is not the board's formal authority, but the use it makes of its authority. The question is whether the board is wise in the traditions of academic governance and legitimate behavior when program approval issues are contested.

We have pointed out that matters of individual autonomy tend to govern discussions of course content and teaching. A type of "senatorial" courtesy prevails in these matters. Gaff and Puzon (2000) made the argument that this individual autonomy does not add up to corporate institutional accountability. The integrity of programs, like the content of the major, relies on the collective authority of the group, usually the department. But in cases of judgment, individual autonomy tends to trump collective authority, giving faculty considerable latitude to interpret what constitutes course content relative to the major. Effective governance requires that the individual freedom to speak without constraint be balanced with the requirement to be responsible for the integrity of programs rather than individual courses.

According to Gaff and Puzon (2000), pressures for institutional accountability require a focus on the education of students and programs of study rather than individual courses. A program is a corporate responsibility, and therefore individual autonomy is not an absolute. The accountability pressure exerted by the market described in Chapter 1 has changed the focus from *what is taught* to *what is learned* and calls into question individual hegemony over the curriculum. Faculty become planners in this regard and not merely individuals operating with complete autonomy.

To illustrate the difference between faculty as course instructors and faculty as planners, we note, as did Gaff and Puzon (2000), that a program offering a degree/certificate typically has at least three features: a set of course requirements, a requirement for a certain amount of learning, and a specified standard of performance. And within an academic major, professional or preprofessional concentration, or general education, a program might have several other features including a set of goals, a substantial introduction to the subject, a core of major courses offered in sequence, a set of related elective courses, and a conclusion or integrative activity. An academic credential or general education program also involves an institutional commitment to offer all course and program requirements so that students can complete their degrees in a timely manner.

Institutional governance typically requires that, in the case of degree programs or major concentrations, the institution, usually in the form of a governing-board credential/diploma, certifies that the individual has completed a *program* of study. This certification, along with the institutional resource commitment to provide all program components in a timely manner, makes a program of study a corporate responsibility. If a program of study is defined as "any activity or collection of activities of the institution that consumes resources (dollars, people, space, equipment, time)" (Dickeson 1999, 44), then the scope of the required resource commitment is more apparent.

This broader view of what constitutes a program is a challenge to the faculty-centered view of academic program governance and is the principal challenge represented by the market forces and other factors discussed in Chapter 1. To quote Gaff and Puzon in some detail:

> However defined, the program of study is necessarily *a corporate responsibility*. It is designed and approved by the governance system of an institution or by one of its units. By definition, the educational program imposes expectations on faculty members; each individual has the responsibility to contribute to the success of the program, regardless of his or her own personal or professional preferences. Although faculty members absolutely need freedom and autonomy, their autonomy is not absolute. It is constrained, minimally, by their obligation to contribute to the educational program(s) for which they are hired.
>
> But the most important challenge to the faculty-centered view of academic governance is the changing instructional paradigm … *from teaching to learning*. This shift in thinking called for a change from a focus on the faculty member and her teaching to a focus on students and their learning. This implies that the faculty member, rather than being the primary actor in the teaching-learning enterprise, plays an instrumental role to facilitate, assist, encourage, and otherwise promote student learning…. To an extent not anticipated when faculty governance roles were being formulated, faculty collectively are being held responsible by accrediting agencies for student

learning. Today they need to be more purposeful in how they, as a collective, design and implement a course of study that achieves high levels of student learning. (Gaff and Puzon 2000, 8–9)

In short, we have a new paradigm, a new set of principles for governance. According to Massy (2003, 308), "higher education's strategic agendum can be stated in one sentence: Colleges and universities need to improve their core competency in education." He identifies an expanded set of quality principles, among which are to define educational quality in terms of student outcomes; to focus on the process of teaching, learning, and student assessment; and to strive for coherence in curricular and educational processes. For the reader interested in implementation, Massy (2003, 314–344) has a rather extensive conversation about how to develop an agenda for improving the educational core. Dickeson (1999, 54) recommends important criteria for the meaningful prioritization of programs. And Meacham and Gaff (2006) make the case that an institution's mission statement should reflect its vision and expectations for undergraduate education.

We conclude this discussion of corporate responsibility and accountability by observing that the responsibility of the faculty as a whole for the degree program as a whole has become a "political" imperative. Accreditors require student learning assessment, and legislators have performance expectations that go beyond what a faculty member believes he or she has a responsibility to teach. The Association of American Colleges and Universities (AAC&U, 2006) recently adopted a statement that extends historical conceptions of academic freedom to include "responsibilities for the holistic education of students ... the key to improvement is clarity about the larger purposes of academic freedom and about the educational responsibilities it is designed to advance."

It is not an exaggeration to say that the governance relationships among boards, administration, and faculty in the next few decades will be challenged by the requirement for evaluation/accountability based on student learning and performance. Two special problems emerge from this reality. First, why can't students graduate on time? And second, why can't credits transfer more freely across institutions? Such issues can quickly impinge on the faculty's hegemony over the curriculum and result in big governance issues.

ACCOUNTABILITY AND THE CURRICULUM
Graduation Rates

Many external actors or stakeholders attuned to market forces tend to believe that graduation rates are a reasonable measure of institutional performance and accountability. This view is stressed in a report by The Education Trust:

America's colleges and universities have a serious and deep-rooted problem: far too many students who enter our higher education system fail to get a degree. Even among the students most likely to succeed—those who begin

> their college career as full-time freshmen in four-year colleges and universities—only six out of every ten of them on average get a B.A. within six years. This translates into over a *half a million* collegians every year, a group disproportionately made up of low income and minority students, who fall short of acquiring the credentials, skills and knowledge they seek. (Carey 2004, 1)

This report goes on to argue that this is a national problem because, as economies in other nations mature and evolve, external job pressure is creeping further and further up the economic skills ladder. The earnings of young adults with four-year degrees or higher have increased over the last 20 years relative to their peers with less education. And the gap in earnings between college degree holders and those with some college but no degree or only a high school education has widened. The annual earnings of those without a high school diploma or its equivalent have declined (USDOE 2004).

Colleges and universities have long argued that using six-year graduation rates as a performance indicator does not reflect the extreme variability involved in the educational enterprise. First, graduation rates vary considerably among institutions; they range from as low as 20 or 30 percent in some institutions with nonselective admission requirements to 70 or 80 percent or higher at more selective independent colleges (Barefoot 2003). Further, the three-year community college graduation rate required to be reported to the federal government does not reflect the basic mission of these institutions. Community colleges tout their ability to help students understand the level of education needed to meet their career objectives—short-term training or preparation for transfer to another institution to complete a degree. These institutions also help students understand the level of education they are capable of achieving, and that level might not involve completion of a degree. These "cooling out" functions are a legitimate part of the mission of community colleges and are not reflected in statistics anchored in the percentage of students who complete associate degrees within a specified time frame.

Finally, some students never intend to graduate from either a two- or four-year college. They attend the institution of their choice to get away from home, to mature as individuals, and for a variety of other reasons that reflect the complex nature of social maturation. In Chapter 1 we made the case that one of the profound pressures of the market is the growth in enrollments. As higher education has become the norm for high school graduates, we can assume that increasing numbers of students are enrolling with far more diverse intentions than the traditional goal of completing a baccalaureate degree in four years.

It is clear that the factors that influence graduation rates are not simple and may be related to such fundamentals as the lack of courses owing to inadequate public funding for higher education, the increased difficulty of paying for an ever more expensive college education, the increased mobility of students, and the large number of part-time students who, for whatever reason, are not pursuing degrees full time. On the other hand, it is a legitimate question to ask what part of graduation rates might be under the control of an individual system or campus and, further, what governance arrangements promote student learning and access to predictable progression toward graduation. Our consulting and practical experiences lead us to profile two institutions where faculty governance practices have resulted in barriers to progression toward a degree.

One major midwestern state university of more than 12,000 students reflects this problem. The institution has a strong faculty union that coexists with the faculty senate. The graduation rate is about 40 percent for this comprehensive institution. In another western state university of some 5,000 to 7,000 students, the graduation rate is approximately 30 percent.

In both institutions the faculty determine the class schedule, and they have a practice of scheduling major courses before they schedule general education courses. Among the students, those with seniority based on accrued credits are allowed to register first. Therefore, many underclassmen are forced to accumulate credits before they can get into the basic courses needed to meet the institution's general education requirements. The problem is exacerbated by the fact that the degrees of freedom that exist in developing the overall class schedule are used to schedule major courses, and the scheduling of general education classes suffers as a result.

Students constantly complain that they are unable to get the general education classes that are required because they have not accumulated sufficient credits. In consequence, many students delay the completion of their general education requirements until they are well grounded in the major—a situation that destroys the basic assumption that general education requirements establish the foundation for advanced study in a major. The result can be the real example of an English major who, having completed all of her major requirements, enrolled one final semester for the sole purpose of taking English 100.

Other qualitative and resource issues can also arise. Because many faculty members prefer to teach students majoring in their discipline or graduate students, the teaching of general education classes can be relegated to part-time instructors or people not on the tenure track. This can lead to questions from parents and others about whether students are getting the benefit of the institution's best faculty. And certain academic practices prevail in some institutions that operate as follows. In underenrolled disciplines—areas that may not offer popular majors—general education courses become the basis for maintaining the department/program's resource profile. If this practice is widespread and the institution offers a cafeteria of courses *acceptable* for the same general education requirement(s), an unintended consequence can be an excessive number of low-enrolled courses and a strain on resources that might be better used to offer the core courses required of every student.

These are problems that require governance modification, have resource allocation implications, and are a basic concern to boards and administration as well as faculty. Matching the institution's need to provide degree paths that match the reality of student registrations with the faculty's hegemony over the curriculum is a major issue in governance arrangements. Again, according to

Gaff and Puzon (2000), the administration and board are held accountable for prudent and effective use of resources, but have little authority over the curriculum. On the other hand, faculty have authority over the curriculum, but little or no accountability for the institution or program as a whole. This may constitute the "what, me worry?" approach to governance. When authority is not combined with responsibility, a classic governance dilemma prevails.

A second major issue involving the governance of the curriculum occurs when students attempt to transfer credits between institutions. We consider this subject by focusing on the case of student transfer at a public state system of higher education (identified here as the University). This system had one governing board and a president who also was the head of the main campus. Four-year campus heads reported directly to the president, and the two-year campuses reported to a system executive who reported to the president. We use this case to illustrate how changing student behavior and accountability forces exert pressure on the faculty's traditional hegemony over the curriculum. The result is a big issue; the political model and rules of advocacy take over and trump what might appear as rational and logical proposals.

Student Transfer Case

For more than 30 years, the two- and four-year campuses that comprise the University system sought with varying degrees of success to make student and credit transfer within the system as smooth as possible. The process used to coordinate these activities was referred to as *articulation*. University transfer agreements typically specified the level, kind, and number of courses taken at one campus that would be accepted by another campus as fulfilling various core, general education, major, or overall credit requirements.

More than 30 years ago an articulation policy was developed by a University committee with membership from the two- and four-year campuses. It was approved by the research campus faculty senate, the faculties and administration of the two-year institutions, and the system president and was shared with the governing board for information. It established the parameters for student and credit transfer and served as the foundation for future policies.

Also in these earlier years, an agreement between the system executive for the two-year campuses and the dean for arts and sciences at the research campus established a process for articulating two-year courses with the core requirements of the research campus. This agreement was based primarily on certification by the system executive for the two-year campuses that courses merited transfer.

Some 18 years after the original articulation policy was established, its main provisions and those of the agreement between the two- and four-year campuses were incorporated into a formal system transfer policy. The senior academic staff officers from the two- and four-year campuses took lead responsibility for codifying the provisions of this policy, and it was promulgated by the president after extensive review and discussion with faculty senates and administrators from each campus. It formalized the existing course-by-course articulation process and established a process for the periodic joint review of courses, an articulation coordinating council for the system, and system faculty standing committees. These committees reviewed courses in the major areas of undergraduate education and recommended to the campuses those to be used to meet general education requirements. Acceptance of the committee's recommendations then rested with the campuses.

Over the years, it was not uncommon for students who encountered transfer disappointments or problems to share their concerns with senior executives, presidents, members of the governing board, and legislators. As a result, what might otherwise be thought of as internal academic matters spilled over into the public policy arena. In response, the system found it necessary to report to the board and legislative committees on the status of articulation and transfer. Assurances to the governing board and legislators about efforts to make articulation work did not diminish their interest in this subject.

Continuing concerns about the effectiveness of articulation caused the administration to seek the expertise of a nationally recognized consultant to examine university student record data bases to determine what could be learned about transfer and articulation issues based on actual student behavior. Major findings of this study were that (1) students were transferring from the two-year institutions to the main campus of the system, but the numbers flowing through this pipeline were small compared to fully articulated state systems elsewhere; (2) students who completed an associate of arts (AA) degree before transfer appeared to perform better than those who did not; (3) prior two-year experience within the system, and especially if the AA degree was completed, appeared particularly beneficial for various ethnic minorities who went on to attend the research campus; and (4) the university had little at risk if it moved to recognize the AA degree offered by the two-year campuses as fulfilling the general education core requirements of the research campus. These findings, particularly the last, received a lukewarm response from the main campus, and little was done in response to the consultant's recommendations. The matter was placed on the back burner.

Several years later a new University president arrived; he spent his initial weeks visiting each campus and meeting with faculty, students, and community leaders. The concerns shared with the new president during these visits clearly suggested that past University efforts to improve articulation were not enough. On completing his visits, the president asked why the University did not recognize and honor its own degrees. In particular, he wanted to know why the AA degree offered by the two-year institutions was not being accepted as fulfilling general education requirements at the four-year campuses. These questions were put forward before the new president was briefed on the consultant's earlier findings and recommendations.

Characterizing what needed to be done as a "no-brainer," the new president charged a council (composed of the senior academic staff officers from the two-

and four-year campuses and chaired by a system officer) with the task of drafting a plan and process, including consultation with appropriate academic bodies, that would result in the establishment of a policy designating the AA degree as meeting general education requirements for all University baccalaureate degrees. As it undertook its review, this council realized that governing board policy was silent on the subject of student transfer and unbalanced in that it referenced core requirements at the research campus but made no mention of this matter for other campuses. Two amendments to board policy were drafted. The first provided a broad policy framework that enabled (but did not specify) a common system approach to general education, and the second emphasized the university's commitment to a simple and predictable transfer process that assisted students who could benefit from transfer. Both amendments were well received and, along with a delegation to the president to promulgate appropriate implementing policy, were adopted by the governing board.

The administration prepared a revised policy on transfer and it was shared with the campuses for broad distribution. The major change from existing policy was a provision that would require the acceptance of an AA degree granted by the two-year campuses of the system as fulfilling the general education core requirements at all baccalaureate campuses of the system. Criteria for the AA degree were specified in the policy and were modeled after the research campus general education core. Except for the transfer AA provision, this revision continued campus autonomy over curriculum and degree requirements; it established a network of campus transfer specialists and committed to tracking patterns of student progress across the system.

The revised transfer policy draft received a favorable review by the faculty senates at the University's two-year campuses and at one four-year campus. When it was considered by the faculty senate of the research campus, however, it met with opposition and was referred to a senate standing committee. At an April senate meeting, a request for quorum precluded a positive action that was supported by the senate standing committee. The following month, the senate passed a motion (33 in favor and 2 opposed) that supported the principle of accepting the AA degree as satisfying the research campus core requirements contingent on four conditions: a mechanism for systemwide coordination of the core, enhanced advising, senate (executive committee) involvement in the revision of the final policy, and senate consideration of the final policy. Shortly after this action, the administration forwarded the final draft policy to all faculty senate chairs and in early June received notification from the executive committee of the research campus senate indicating satisfaction with the revisions. As a result of these actions, the three chancellors responsible for the campuses affected by the policy signed an agreement that set forth the basic tenets and initiatives contained in the revised policy.

The policy became final upon promulgation by the president in July, and a follow-up memorandum was sent to the research campus senate summarizing the changes that were and were not made to the revised policy before its promulgation. The research campus senate did not comment on this final policy in the summer or after the beginning of the next term; there was no return communication indicating any further concerns. In August, the president officially established a transfer network (composed of staff that provided transfer assistance/advising at the campus level) and charged it with helping to implement the policy. This action was thought to be responsive to the senate's concern for enhanced advising. Over time, however, it became clear that some members of the network disagreed with major policy components, and these disagreements became major barriers to implementation of a policy that had received faculty senate and administrative approvals.

With the opening of the fall semester, the president acted to support, at their request, an effort by University faculty senate chairs from across the system to reform general education. This action was viewed by the administration as an ideal response to the first condition attached to the research campus approval of the draft policy. This faculty-led project was staffed and supported by the administration, spanned three years, and resulted in agreement in principle on minimum outcomes for five academic skill areas expected of students upon the completion of their general education experience. This agreement was endorsed by faculty senates on all campuses, but it was met with indifference and opposition from leadership of the liberal arts faculty at the research campus and very little resulted from this lengthy effort.

With the promulgation of the revised transfer policy, the administration committed to monitor student progress relative to the policy and to review the policy after a period of implementation. The first of these activities showed that only about 25 percent of spring semester AA graduates transferred to the research campus in the fall and that their grades in their first semester after transfer were equal to those earned in the same semester by juniors who began their careers at the research campus.

Approximately four years after the revised policy was promulgated, in response to issues that were causing difficulty for students and confusion for faculty and staff, the president directed the administration to again update the system transfer policy. The president specifically asked that the update reaffirm the governing board's commitment to make transfer simple and predictable. This review was prompted by the administration's original commitment to review the policy and by concerns at the research campus that the policy was an impediment to regional campus accreditation. Also, the research campus had begun to reject the admission of transfer students from within the system holding an AA degree because a recomputation of the student's overall grade point average didn't meet the research campus's 2.0 admission requirement. These rejections, although few in number, generated considerable controversy.

Again, the system academic council was asked to carry out a policy review. Its members agreed at the outset that they would handle the liaison work with their campuses to communicate and receive feedback on changes to the document. This council considered information and comments from faculty senates, staff, and administrators. In particular, the provisions of a recent resolution from the faculty senate of the research campus were considered. Draft revisions were broadly shared. This revision process took approximately one semester, at the end of which the president promulgated an updated policy.

The revised policy addressed the accreditation issue. Administrators met with the executive director of the regional accrediting association and confirmed their earlier understanding that a University policy directing the acceptance of an AA degree (conferred within the system) as fulfilling the general education core requirements at the baccalaureate campuses of the system was not in conflict with or an impediment to the regional accreditation of the four-year and research institutions.

The revised policy again tried to carefully balance the importance of removing unreasonable barriers to transfer with campus responsibility for determining specific transfer policies and practices consistent with their missions. A key revision to the policy clarified that the AA degree satisfied both general education and admission requirements at the baccalaureate campuses and that the final authority for determining the applicability of liberal arts transfer credit resided with the receiving campus. A number of lead responsibilities and procedures were also clarified, especially the role of the University council on articulation and the importance of faculty involvement on this council.

At this point, it appeared that an important, albeit modest, effort at improving transfer had been completed and now attention could be turned to implementation issues. This turned out to be only partially true. From the administration's point of view, the University transfer policy was about honoring the integrity of one of its degrees and the faculty who designed and delivered it, while continuing to place final authority for determining degree requirements and the acceptance and applicability of credits with receiving campuses and their faculty. Given the small numbers of students who actually sought to transfer with an AA degree and their overall record of success after transfer, the revised policy seemed extraordinarily reasonable.

When the following fall semester opened, however, the research campus faculty senate expressed concern that the resolution they had passed the previous spring had not been given due consideration by the administration in the revision of the University's transfer policy. The administration quickly learned that there was an expectation among some faculty leaders that "consultation" on this matter meant that all of the senate's recommendations would be incorporated in the updated policy. This prompted the administration to prepare a specific summary of how some concerns raised in the senate's resolution were addressed and why others could not be used. Specifically, some recommendations eliminated or weakened longstanding transfer policies, appeared to be based on rationales not grounded in evidence about student achievement or lack thereof, and ignored or discounted the assurance received from the regional accrediting executive that the policy was not in conflict with accreditation requirements.

In general, the senate resolution appeared to have little regard for the legitimate responsibility of a public sector governing board that wanted assurances that system policy was facilitating the transfer of students who wanted the opportunity to begin their college education at one campus and, through productive study, succeed in achieving their educational objectives by graduating from another campus.

In addition to raising concerns that the administration did not give due consideration to their resolution, statements were made in a fall senate meeting at the research campus that the administration did not respond to actions taken by the senate four years earlier when the policy establishing the transfer AA was first promulgated. This caused the administration to revisit the earlier sequence of exchanges between the senate and the administration and provide a written summary of the efforts that were made to respond to senate concerns.

From the perspective of at least some of the faculty at the research campus, an AA transfer policy took away faculty control over the general education requirements for their degree. They interpreted the policy to mean that they had to accept and apply toward the baccalaureate degree all credits and courses numbered above 100 that a student took at a two-year campus in the course of completing an AA degree. In fact, the policy made it clear that the receiving campus did not have to accept the credits for every course used to complete the AA degree, but it did have to accept AA degree completion as fulfilling the general education core requirements at the baccalaureate degree-granting campuses.

When a regional accreditation team visited the research campus the next spring, it appeared to take up the cause of those who had opposed the various revisions to the system transfer policy. The team raised with the administration concerns about faculty authority over the curriculum. This occurred despite the campus senate's positive action on this policy and earlier assurances from the accrediting body that the policy was not in conflict with or an impediment to regional accreditation.

In the several years that followed, the research campus engaged in a revision of its general education requirements. The broad outcome of this effort was positive for all transfer students, making the core more flexible and reducing total requirements. An indirect consequence was to reduce the advantage previously associated with attaining an AA degree before transfer within the system. And now, more than 10 years later, the University's student transfer policies continue to be discussed and revised.

Case Dynamics

The student transfer case sheds light on governance claims that arise and the consequences of these claims when dealing with academic programs.

Overlapping Claims

Within the higher education community, it is not well understood or accepted that responsibility for some academic programs, especially general education, must extend beyond the boundaries of disciplines and even campuses. As demonstrated in this case, the lack of agreement on this fundamental premise resulted in a big, messy issue and years of debate and controversy.

When administrators venture to deal with issues in areas of responsibility traditionally viewed by faculty to be their sole domain, solutions that may appear rational and reasonable in administrative circles may be trumped by faculty concerned about protecting their authority and control over the curriculum. When the boundaries between traditional authority domains are crossed, a big issue will emerge and the likelihood of political behavior will increase. One lesson learned is that there are no "no-brainers" in higher education when administrators, no matter how well intentioned, attempt to deal with matters affecting curricula.

The mobility of students—60 percent attend more than one institution and 35 percent attend more than two (Hoover 2006)—and the role of two-year institutions within a system of higher education raise the governance issue of whether the faculty's dominion over the curriculum should be confined to campus boundaries or should be shared with faculty from feeder institutions. Two-year campuses tend eventually to model their general education requirements after those at the large receiving schools to which they send their students. But they will not accept a lack of respect for their degrees based on assumptions about quality that are not consistent with student performance.

Faculty Claims

Faculty protection of what they understand to be their exclusive right to determine all aspects of general education course and credit requirements at their campus can trump student achievement data that demonstrates the reasonableness of honoring a degree credential from another campus as fulfilling those requirements. This sense of exclusivity can be so strong that its advocates will interpret policy requirements in ways not consistent with stated intentions. Such advocacy is typical behavior within a political framework and demonstrates the importance of understanding that debates within the academy take on a political character when a big issue emerges. Mathews (2005) provides an enlightened treatment of the unexamined assumptions about quality in higher education. His analysis challenges the assumption that the learning taking place at one institution is inherently better than that at another based on factors such as faculty reputation or institutional type and status.

Student Claims

The mobile nature of student populations places stress on the faculty's exclusive dominion over some program and curricular matters. The academy has not mastered reconciling legitimate faculty control over curricula with the legitimate needs of student populations who take courses at multiple institutions. These students, parents, government officials, and the general public express a legitimate concern when they question the need to repeat course work; they often express a fear that they are paying for degree credits twice.

Governing Board Claims

Boards and legislators expect systems of higher education to function in a way that permits students to combine course work from multiple institutions (with different but legitimate perspectives on general education) in a manner that does not result in an extended time to graduate. Boards view this as their corporate responsibility, and legislators view it as a public good for which they have some responsibility. Forums that bring all parties (faculty, administrators, boards, and legislators) together to share views and perhaps even reach consensus on governance arrangements that honor the legitimate claims of each party would be a worthwhile investment of resources.

Role of Accreditors

Accreditors can send mixed signals when it comes to the authority and responsibility for policies relating to student and course transfer within a state system of higher education. In their effort to advance legitimate state interests while protecting faculty prerogatives, they can appear to come down on both sides of an issue. This can contribute to the politicization of an issue. Savvy governance participants know that claims associated with threats to the accreditation status of their institution will draw support for an advocate's position.

Fluid Decisions and Implementation

Decisions are rarely final and participation is fluid. Committed individuals can ensure that no decision is final. The student transfer case is an excellent example of how decisions *flow*—a matter can be returned to the forefront of debate long after some (usually administrators) assume that resolution has taken place. It takes agreement among a large number of faculty leaders to move a major academic program policy forward, but the advocacy of a few committed individuals can turn the matter into a big issue, give it a political character, and delay or perhaps halt approval efforts. And even if the majority faculty voice does not agree with a minority faculty view, the minority can potentially influence the outcome by raising process issues (e.g., the legitimacy of administrative and even their own senate governance processes).

Implementation is everything. Policy development and approval processes can be rendered ineffective if those charged with implementation presume, without challenge, to subvert the intent of a policy. In the student transfer case, faculty senate and administration approval did not constrain those responsible for transcript evaluation from effectively changing the terms of the policy in the implementation process. Thus the gap between policy and implementation in a large decentralized system can prevent a policy from meeting its desired outcomes.

SUMMARY

If there is a hierarchy of difficulty within the art of university governance, governance of academic matters must surely be at or near the top. Universities may be *for the student*, but they are definitely *by the faculty*. Making and implementing academic decisions about matters that cross legitimate claims and become corporate issues test all shared governance partners to reconsider whether the domains they carefully defend are in the best interests of those the institution serves—students. The faculty's control of the curriculum, the board's responsibility for program oversight, and the administration's responsibility to account for the wise use of resources can all come into conflict and lead to some of the most wicked problems and long-lasting and corrosive relationships.

This chapter began by detailing the evolution of academic programs. They tend to evolve through a complex process wherein faculty autonomy is sacrosanct. Programs emerge in response to faculty and student interests, new funding opportunities, and the changing demands of the public. We spend a good deal of time showing that the curriculum as a whole is a corporate responsibility and that this "wholeness" is becoming a political imperative in the current accountability debates.

Through an analysis of a credit transfer debate, we have seen how reaching agreement on actions that facilitate degree attainment for mobile student populations challenges all governance partners—to examine their domains of authority and consider how they can protect their essential spheres of control, tread lightly on others, and work to aim the pointy end of their common ship in directions that benefit students and society. We have also seen how the politics of advocacy can drive wedges within faculty ranks and between faculty and administrators. In Chapter 5 we discuss the importance of avoiding wedges in the president-provost relationship.

CHAPTER 5

President-Provost Governance Relations

Few presidents can be much better than their provosts and even fewer can be much worse—at least, not for very long!

Previous chapters examined the dynamics of faculty governance and how governing boards operate. In this chapter we turn our attention to another key component in the art of governance, the administration—specifically, the relationship between a president and the chief academic officer (CAO). A version of the quote that opens this chapter has been used to describe the relationship between presidents and their boards (AGB 1984, 89). We believe the insight expressed therein also applies to the relationship between presidents and provosts.

Academic leadership is thought to be the major task of a president. In practice, it is the responsibility of everyone—board, president, chief academic officers, deans, faculty, and staff. Presidents lead in academic affairs through a team of actors of which the CAO is the key. Developing an administrative cadre with a sense of common vision and the continuity so necessary for effective governance is a chief ingredient in the recipe for practicing the art of governance. The administrative cadre we refer to consists chiefly of the president and the provost, but in practice includes the various deans and, depending on the context of the institution, department chairs.

In this chapter, we refer to the CAO as the provost, recognizing that other commonly used titles for this position are vice president for academic affairs and dean of instruction. We explore the nature of relationships between the chief executive officer, referred to here as president, and the CAO/provost. The president-provost partnership is not well understood, but its dynamics are crucial to the political nature of governance described in this book.

The chapter begins with a brief description of the roles of the president and the provost. Several cases demonstrate how difficult it is in practice to develop coherent institutional leadership between the president and provost when their time together is short. The case of Mythical State University is used to illustrate a president's attempt to exert leadership in planning without the existence of a permanent provost. Some of the tough problems presidents and provosts encounter as they work together are discussed, and the chapter concludes with observations about best practices.

THE ACADEMIC PRESIDENT

Crowley (1994, 1) has written a thorough summary of the literature about the presidency. He points out that images of presidents abound and are rich and provocative. These images include superman, hero, titan, statesman, visionary, gladiator, peacekeeper, pilot, and pathbreaker. Such images are often contrasted with the less grand characterizations as boss, broker, catalyst, communicator, moderator, and mediator. Another level down, metaphorically, is the portrayal of the president as a foreman, bellhop, zookeeper, lightning rod, divining rod, chemist, chameleon, clerk, or gambler. Even less kind appraisals have considered the president as a hack, bottleneck, nuisance, villain, autocrat, menace, scapegoat, or illegitimate force.

The job itself has been variously described as "necessary, conspicuous, unique, laborious, precious, precarious ... a dog's life ... and no way for an adult to make a living." Crowley goes on to suggest that those who hold the job need to have courage and judgment, be bold, compassionate, intelligent, prudent, patient, resilient, and responsive, have nerves like sewer pipes, be good listeners, have one blind eye and one deaf ear, plus white hair for that look of experience, and hemorrhoids for that look of concern. And they should be lucky (Crowley 1994, 2).

In practice, the duties of fundraising, lobbying, public relations, and management can consume more of the president's time and energy than academic matters. In a 2001 survey of American college presidents, Corrigan (2002, 34) reported on the top issues occupying presidents' time. Presidents of public institutions ranked academic issues eighth; private sector presidents ranked academic issues sixth. For both sectors, academic issues ranked poorly in terms of their priority for a president's time behind fundraising, planning, budgeting, board relations, and personnel issues. For presidents of public institutions, community relations and relationships with legislators and political officials also occupied more of a president's time than did academic issues.

When asked for a list of the greatest challenges confronting them, presidents overall ranked relationships with faculty as number one, well ahead of relationships with legislators and governing boards. Public sector presidents most often identified relations with legislators and policymakers as their greatest challenge, followed by those with faculty (Corrigan 2002, 33–34).

Here we have the horns of the dilemma. When it comes to how they spend their time, presidents find that they spend it on many issues other than academic ones, yet they acknowledge that one of the most challenging issues confronting them is academic—their relationships with faculty. The competing priorities represented by this dilemma make the president-provost relationship critical. As presidents have less and less time to devote to academic matters, they need provosts who can guide faculty through tough academic issues. Birnbaum captures the importance of multiple sources of leadership:

> College presidents can be important. When they are perceived by their constituents as competent, legitimate, value-driven, of complex mind, and open to influence, presidents can be a vital source of leadership and a force for institutional renewal. At the same time, presidents are not the only source of campus leadership, and colleges can improve even when presidents fail. In an academic institution, leadership can be provided by others, and attention can be focused by history, culture, and training. (Birnbaum 1992, 151)

Birnbaum (1992, 171–172) goes on to state that "the major problem of presidential leadership in a turbulent environment is getting people to share a common sense of reality when, as a result of that environment, everyone's head hurts too much to think about it." In our view, turbulent environments are a given; they require presidential leadership of major academic matters to be a team activity, articulated most meaningfully through provosts and deans. It takes time together to build a coherent team of academic leaders. And the larger, more complex, and public an institution, the more difficult it is to build and retain such a team for the duration of a 5- to 10-year presidency. A president's impact on academic affairs can be enhanced or seriously diminished depending on the strength of the relationship with the provost.

THE PROVOST

It is then clear that the partnership between the president and the CAO is absolutely crucial to effective institutional governance. The president cannot shirk his or her responsibility, for the buck stops at the highest level, but the provost and deans have line responsibility for faculty relationships and morale. Martin and others (1997, 5) report that the following groupings of responsibilities demand the time and skills of deans and provosts in descending order of importance: faculty relations and morale; recruitment of faculty; curriculum work; budget, promotions, and personnel evaluation; committee work; routine administration; and student counseling.

The CAO is usually regarded as the lead faculty voice in administrative councils and can be pivotal in assessing the faculty's readiness for change and preparing the political ground for presidential initiatives (Bornstein 2003, 154). As such, the CAO role is varied and requires dealing with competing and conflicting demands. Martin and others (1997, 17–20) argue that there are at least 10 different roles that provosts play in performing their responsibilities: an expert with ambiguity, a champion of new technologies, an institutional entrepreneur, a student affairs advocate, a savvy fundraiser, a supporter of selected excellence, a legal interpreter, a public intellectual, a shaper of new consensus, and a visionary pragmatist.

Our experience on the topic indicates that trust and a mutual attitude of support are key ingredients in president-provost relationships. The ideal foundation for trust and support is expressed in a shared vision for an institution's future and an overall consensus on actions needed to implement that vision. Presidents typically take the lead when it comes to the overall goals to be pursued during their tenure. But it usually falls to the provost to figure out how to translate goals into actions—how to get things done. And it takes time, as we will demonstrate in Chapter 6, to translate a vision into a plan embraced by a university community, and even more time to implement a plan.

A successful president-provost team requires time together. The importance of the constancy needed in the president-provost roles to achieve coherent and effective working relationships is often overlooked. In reflecting on his time as a provost, Paradise captures our experience: "Instituting strategic planning, resource-allocation procedures, accountability initiatives, and the like takes time. Without several years to develop, refine, and implement, little real improvement takes place. Staying on the job for only three years leaves little room for constancy" (Paradise 2004). We offer case material from four different institutions to shed light on how long presidents and provosts serve together. We will leave it to future researchers to determine how representative these cases are of practices across the profession.

TIME ON THE JOB TOGETHER

In the first case, an acting president assumed the role when the previous president died in office. Before becoming the acting president, this individual had been the acting provost for only a few months. When elevated into the acting presidency, he appointed the dean of the graduate school as acting provost. This former dean of the graduate school remained as acting provost when the new, permanent president assumed office. The person who had served as acting president then became a vice president and continued to serve the university for years.

One of the new president's first tasks was to assess the process to be used in the search for a permanent provost. After the appropriate academic amenities were observed, a search committee was appointed and a permanent provost was selected and took office a year after the president had taken office. The former acting provost retired from the university. Unfortunately, the new provost died nine months later. An assistant provost was appointed as the acting provost and served for a year while a second search process took place. This individual eventually received the appointment as permanent provost. The point of this chronology is that it was three years before the permanent president had the opportunity to work with a permanent provost for more than a short period of time. And to complicate issues of coherence even more, the president moved on to another presidency 18 months later.

In a second case, a president took office in an institution where the former acting provost had been elevated to acting president when the previous president resigned. With the appointment of a new president, the acting president returned to the acting provost position and was in that role for about a year. The appropriate search mechanisms were put in place, and a permanent provost was identified. Unfortunately, this individual passed away shortly thereafter and an acting provost, from the ranks of the vice presidents, was again appointed. The provost's job was filled by a variety of people during the first three or four years of the new president's tenure.

In a third case, a president resigned to take another presidency. The provost then became acting president and was an active candidate for the permanent job. When he was not chosen, he resigned as provost and went on sabbatical. The new president appointed an acting provost and conducted the obligatory search. A new provost finally took office nearly two years after the president had assumed office.

In a fourth case, the president and provost at an independent institution served together for over a decade. When the president took office, the university was in a deficit condition and certain "tough" decisions had to be made to put the university on a financially secure footing. Ten years later the academic plan had been in place for some time and the university was in the throes of mounting its first major fundraising campaign. The president and the provost were perceived to be working in harmony in the implementation of a grand plan to elevate the university to its next tier of excellence.

The first three cases provide insight into how difficult it is to have a strong voice representing faculty interests and on major academic matters within the cadre of senior officers when the provost position has revolving-door incumbents. The fourth case demonstrates the institutional benefits that can result when there is continuity in the tenure of presidents and provosts. The institutional leadership situations in the first three cases present a series of dilemmas about how presidents and provosts can work together when they do not serve together for long periods of time. The dilemmas are particularly acute when the president feels that he or she must move ahead even in the absence of a permanent provost. The case of Mythical State University illustrates this point succinctly.

MYTHICAL STATE UNIVERSITY

Events at Mythical State

President Jones was appointed president of Mythical State University (MSU) after a year-long search during which the provost served as acting president and a senior faculty member was appointed acting provost. The acting president was a candidate for the presidency; he was not appointed and left the university. The acting provost stayed on during the search for his replacement.

During his first year in office, the president concluded that he had little confidence in the ability of the acting provost to make the hard choices facing MSU. As a result the president took a stronger role in directing academic affairs than he thought wise. He hoped that, when a permanent provost was appointed, he could resume his presidential duties and a more traditional president-provost relationship would develop. In the meantime, the president moved ahead to revise the MSU mission and goals statements. To improve the university's status, the president committed the institution to join a new accreditation effort. The president argued that this would further clarify the university's role in undergraduate education and help the institution reinforce its "mission-centeredness."

In the previous two years MSU suffered significant budget cuts from the state, accompanied by a precipitous rise in tuition. Because MSU's enrollments remained stable while those at all other public institutions in the state increased, it appeared to some that MSU's budget cuts were more severe.

In addition, the systemwide chancellor that hired President Jones retired, and the new chancellor's commitment to President Jones was somewhat speculative. Also, the faculty union contract was in the midst of being renegotiated. The current contract was to expire at the close of the academic year.

Finally, the president determined that a new strategic plan was needed to assist with short-term budget cuts and to plan the fiscal future of MSU. To undertake the preparation of this strategic plan, the president appointed a special strategic planning committee whose task was to render advice on both short- and long-term priorities and to develop a plan for the university community to debate.

The appointment of this special strategic planning committee galvanized the MSU faculty senate in opposition. Faculty argued that the president was doing too much too soon, that the faculty and the senate had not been properly consulted about the need for a plan, the need to move ahead with this new accreditation status, the need to have a new mission statement, and especially the need to appoint a special committee rather than using the existing senate committee on university planning to accomplish the purposes outlined by the president.

The president's review of the matter uncovered three important facts. First, the committee referred to by the faculty was the University Planning Committee, and it had atrophied over the years into a body that only dealt with issues involving the physical master plan for the campus. In reality, there was no committee that dealt with academic planning as such, although this function was referenced in the documents creating the University Planning Committee. And, although the University Planning Committee was perceived by the faculty to be a senate committee, it was actually a joint committee of the senate and the administration.

In its first deliberations, the newly appointed strategic planning committee was confused as to how it might play an advisory role in determining short-term priorities in order to handle the university's budget deficit for the remainder of the current academic year and the next year. They understood that the plan they were asked to develop would have a three- to five-year scenario and would involve debate about fundamental directions to be taken given the great volatility in the world external to the university.

As a result of this confusion, the faculty senate passed a resolution and instructed its leadership to negotiate a new *modus operandi* with the president. The resolution demanded that proper procedures be followed in the development of a plan, including the opportunity for all members of the university community to participate.

Because of the implied threat of a vote of no confidence, the president felt he had no option but to agree with the senate's demand to develop a new set of understandings about the appropriate processes and criteria to be followed in making important campus decisions.

The president prepared a discussion memorandum that was widely circulated on campus and entitled "The Roles and Responsibilities for Strategic Planning and

Budgeting." The major issue was to clarify the locus of responsibility for advising and working with the administration on short- and long-term budgeting and planning. It pointed out that the University Planning Committee, which was actually a joint committee of the faculty senate and the administration, had been historically charged with the duties of developing guidelines for program, fiscal, and facilities planning, including the allocation of resources, the development of biennial and annual budgets, and the establishment of priorities in capital construction and maintenance. In practice, over the last 15 years, this committee focused on only that aspect of its charge relating to physical facilities and capital improvements.

In general the faculty senate and other members of the community agreed with the president's analysis but argued that, now that academic planning was a "big issue," it was time for the regular MSU governance mechanism to take it over. To work out these differences, the president laid out three alternatives for discussion by the campus community.

The first alternative was for the senate and the administration to change the bylaws to drastically narrow the charge of the existing University Planning Committee so that the work of the new strategic planning committee could proceed as planned. Both parties agreed that it would not be appropriate to be in violation of university bylaws, no matter how expedient it might seem.

The second option was for the senate and administration to conclude that the bylaws not be changed because it was such a tedious process. This option would disband the special planning committee, and the University Planning Committee would now engage in the full range of its charge as specified in the bylaws. This option would also include some modification in the membership of the University Planning Committee.

The third option was for the senate and the administration to develop a written agreement based on the roles of both the University Planning Committee and the new special strategic planning committee. A new planning committee would be established; it would be in place through the development and implementation of the strategic plan, a period expected to span the next five or six years. This agreement would also specify a general plan for determining the membership of the new committee, with an understanding that specific membership would be a subject for discussion between the parties.

In the informal conversation about the desired course of action, the fact that the faculty union contract was in the process of being negotiated became a complicating factor. Many of the faculty members on the union's bargaining committee were active in the senate. Several of the issues expected to be discussed as part of the planning efforts were also being presented at the bargaining table.

Case Lessons

The MSU experience illustrates several lessons about president-provost relationships. First, lack of trust in the provost led the president to assume a more direct role in dealing with the faculty than he thought was desirable. This meant that there was no credible buffer between the president and the faculty and caused the president to use a lot of the "honeymoon" period typically afforded new presidents to deal with procedural matters. When this happens, the all-too-common misunderstandings about how activities were handled in the past or about proposed procedural details can result in ill will that can overtake a president's broader institutional agenda.

Second, the MSU president was dealing with both a union and a senate, and there was substantial overlap in both the informal and formal membership of these bodies. When presidents find themselves in this situation, they will perceive that including senate leaders in the confidential conversations necessary for various planning and budget decisions will be difficult, if not impossible. Effective provosts, because of their more daily involvement with faculty leaders, may be able to maneuver through some of the hurdles of such an environment, but in general the shared governance arrangements that all parties support in principle will likely be short-changed.

Third, the absence of an effective MSU provost rapidly drained the president's capacity to deal with issues in areas other than academic affairs. Presidents who do not give adequate attention to pressing external and legislative affairs risk losing needed support for both their academic and broader institutional priorities.

In summary, the MSU case and the other president-provost situations discussed here demonstrate that it may not be common for a president-provost "team" to have the time together needed to develop the working trust and coherence so necessary to pursue the art of governance effectively. The dynamics of this relationship deserve further discussion.

PRESIDENT-PROVOST DYNAMICS

The literature, our experience, and some national conversations lead us to make a variety of observations about the dynamics of the relationship between presidents and provosts as institutional leaders.

Importance of Mutual Support

The partnership between a president and provost has both its public and private mutual support elements. Internal stakeholders will watch public interactions between the two with great interest. If it is obvious that they don't like each other or disagree, it will affect faculty and administrative morale and will threaten their ability to implement proposed actions. If the provost is perceived as unable to persuade the president on academic matters, deans and faculty will tend to end-run directly to the president or the board and thereby exacerbate the relationship.

Academic issues for which provosts have lead responsibility are among the most vexing that an institution has to deal with. For example, in executive or public sessions of the board the provost's areas of responsibility are likely to be the ones most criticized for being troublesome and costly (new program developments, legal settlements, or expensive new hires). At such times presidents who have agreed to bring such matters forward must publicly support their provosts' actions.

In our discussion with provosts and presidents, they agree that a certain amount of personal "whine time" is necessary, but it has to occur in private. The importance of an opportunity for presidents and provosts to vent in private cannot be overestimated. It is inevitable that disagreements will occur, and the issue is how they are dealt with when they do. Frequent private meetings on both a social and professional level are essential for discussion of such issues. The delicate nature of the relationship requires that these two leaders have enough time together in private to be in tune with each other's personal idiosyncrasies, shortcomings, and strengths and thus build the necessary capital for a unified public handling of matters on which they may not entirely agree.

Understanding Each Other's Interests

Presidents tend to be more interested in outcomes and provosts in process. It helps if both leaders understand this reality. The president's time is likely to be taken up by a variety of activities, some of which are not in the attention span of most provosts—fundraising, legislative relations, and dealing with boards. Provosts need to be accepting of these presidential responsibilities. On the other hand, the art of being a good provost involves working through the processes of academic governance with the deans and faculty. Presidents need to appreciate the amount of time a provost needs to "work the process" and be sensitive to the reality that there is no quicker way to kill any kind of reform or policy implementation than for opponents to argue that the process was not timely or legitimate.

Another wrinkle on the president-provost relationship is the fact that, at some institutions, the chief financial officer and the provost have to work out the balance between financial and academic priorities. For example, it is not unusual for the financial-administrative side of the house to argue that, once academic priorities are set, their offices take charge of the budget and operational prioritizing needed to achieve stated priorities. This frustrates provosts who believe that they and other academics ought to participate equally in any kind of operational planning effort. When these two can't agree, the president is put in the position of having to choose an appropriate course of action, often perceived as "choosing up sides." The result is a strain on the president's relationship with two key leaders.

This point about clarity as to *who does what* was stressed in a forum presentation by the presidents and provosts of three independent colleges at the 2004 meeting of the American Association of Colleges and Universities. The issue was raised as to whether it was dangerous for presidents to have served previously as provosts. It was observed that one of the tasks of new presidents is to remember that he or she is no longer the provost and the details of academic affairs are better left to the chief academic officer. For example, the discussants agreed that the provost needs to work directly with the academic affairs committee of the board of trustees.

Many presidents who have been provosts acknowledge that there is a tendency for them to work the details of academic affairs more than might be the case for the domains represented by other vice presidents or administrators.

When Presidents and Provosts Disagree

The situation in which the president and provost don't agree is so critical that it requires further discussion. When disagreement happens, how can the matter be resolved? We have already suggested that such disagreements need to be worked out in private rather than in public. The three provosts mentioned in the previous paragraph agreed that it is necessary to argue for what is right, but once the decision is made one needs to go along. The personal dynamic is whether or not a president can accept contrary advice and the extent to which one can argue with a president about directions with which the provost does not agree. If provosts are put in the position of having to consistently tell an entrepreneurial president "you can't get away with that," the provost will come to be viewed as the bearer of bad news—a label that will tax any personal relationship. The problem for the provost is how to defend decisions he or she does not agree with so that this disagreement does not become a factor in the implementation process.

On the other hand, experienced presidents realize that there are times when they must accept the provost's recommendations even when they believe it is not the appropriate course of action for the institution. For example, it may well be that a policy has been worked out by the faculty senate and the council of deans and comes to the executive office with a positive recommendation that the provost supports. It is hoped that the president will have been warned that the policy was coming and had an opportunity to express his or her views in private. But the dynamics of academic life don't always result in recommendations presented to a president that the president has had a previous opportunity to review. The president understands that if he or she consistently vetoes or fails to implement such recommendations, the credibility of the provost becomes an issue with the faculty, deans, and the board. Most experienced presidents understand that they must use their authority to veto a provost's recommendations with great restraint.

This latter situation is described by Hayes (1997, 84–86) as follows. A large independent institution faced a period of financial stress, and decisions had to be made about program cuts. The president and the provost had different views about whether programs should be cut in a selective manner or across the board. The president thought undergraduate programs should not be touched and graduate programs should bear the brunt of cutbacks; the provost believed it would be better to retain all programs at a reduced level by across-the-board budget cuts. In presenting the situation to the faculty, the provost's disagreement with the president's strategy was made known, and it became public that the president and the provost did not agree on whether programs should be eliminated. As a result, deans and faculty were reluctant to identify any programs as not essential.

As the financial situation worsened, relations between the president and the provost became vitriolic, and eventually the president felt it necessary to make unilateral decisions about which programs to eliminate. In the end the president lost the esteem of the faculty and the provost was removed. In difficult decisions like these, neither party could have proposed a course of action that would have escaped criticism or campus conflict, but the lack of team leadership by the president and the provost made a bad situation worse.

In another case of a large public institution, the need for restrictions became obvious after several years of severe budget decline. The campus debates about the appropriate actions to be taken were varied and controversial. One faculty committee recommended closing one or two professional schools, thereby protecting the core of the university's programs. During these debates it became clear that several problems needed to be addressed regardless of the current budget situation. These included the need to improve information technology and library resources.

In private, the president and the provost had vigorous debates about the appropriate system of reductions and reallocations to implement the needed reforms. The president was adamant that an across-the-board approach would not be appropriate. He argued that an across-the-board strategy would offend everybody and was politically difficult to implement. The provost was equally adamant that an across-the-board strategy would distribute the pain equally and produce "flexibility money" to fix the problems of information technology and libraries. He argued that the amount to be cut would be in excess of the basic need to meet the budget shortfall, so that substantial reallocation of resources could be accomplished.

The president felt the provost's strategy was a political mistake, but realized that the provost and his staff had become committed to it. The issue became whether to support the provost's recommendation rather than passing judgment on the wisdom of the across-the-board approach. After a frank conversation in which the president agreed not to express his disappointment in this strategy in public, the provost announced a three-year program of across-the-board cuts to be administered through each of the college deans.

The resulting furor was an important ingredient in the campus's evaluation of the provost. Those deans in high priority areas complained that there were no priorities because their programs were absorbing cuts equal to those that were assigned to areas of lesser priority. The provost argued that the reallocation schemes would allow high priority areas to get back some of the money reallocated from the lower priority areas and the campus would be able to move ahead with its priority programs and with enhanced support for information technology and libraries. The campus was in general agreement about the importance of improving the technology and library situations, but it was not in agreement about how this ought to be accomplished. Some continued to argue that the legislature needed to produce the money that was necessary to run a first-class university.

This matter went on for some time and the reallocation of funds into priority areas did occur. The problem was that there were no visible pockets of support. Those deans who were getting lesser cuts or receiving increased support were always angry that they didn't receive more support, and those who were being cut more could never accept the legitimacy of their cuts.

In developments unrelated to this case, the president decided to resign. The provost had become so controversial that he was unacceptable to the incoming president and returned to the faculty soon after the new president took office. Although there are many reasons for changes under new leadership, the budget-cutting scheme was one of the most severe criticisms of the provost and his ability to maintain leadership on the campus.

In the two cases just discussed, the president has a dilemma. The president needs to maintain good relations with the provost and the provost's staff and support the provost in matters relating to the deans and the faculty. On the other hand, how can a president support a set of decisions or processes that go against his or her professional judgment that the proposed course of action will not work? A president's silence in such instances will be perceived as a lack of support for the provost, whereas public support for such measures means sharing responsibility for negative consequences. In both of the cases discussed, the provosts lost their jobs and the presidents lost faculty support and esteem. In situations that require severe budget cuts, it is not clear that presidents and provosts who agree on strategies would fare any better. But when presidents and provosts are not marching to the same drummer, a difficult situation can become personally and professionally more traumatic.

BEST PRACTICES

The literature provides useful summaries of best practices in president-provost relations. Hayes offers seven observations about how a provost can work effectively with the president. In our view, she has captured critical advice on the subject:

- Respect the president's time
- Maintain a policy of no surprises, no secrets
- Be a problem preventer
- If that does not work, be a problem solver
- If that does not work, be a crisis manager
- Provide alternatives when making recommendations
- Support the president's views with deans and faculty. (Hayes 1997, 82)

The importance of president-provost communications cannot be overemphasized. Hayes notes: "Whatever the history and parameters of the relationship, there must be close and frequent communication between these two individuals in order to accomplish the institution's academic agenda. Both have crowded calendars, demanding schedules, and few opportunities for casual interaction, thus regularly scheduled meetings are essential" (Hayes 1997, 82).

Good communication will likely follow if the first principle of good practice is internalized—*recognition that co-leadership is an important element in institutional success*. Heenan and Bennis devote a good deal of attention to the topic in business, sports, and other venues. We believe that much of their analysis applies to the higher education setting. "Co-leadership is not a fuzzy-minded buzzword designed to make non-CEOs feel better about themselves and their workplaces. Rather, it is a tough-minded strategy that will unleash the hidden talent in any enterprise. Above all co-leadership is inclusive, not exclusive. It celebrates those who do the real work, not just a few charismatic leaders, often isolated, who are regally compensated for articulating the organization's vision" (Heenan and Bennis 1999, 5).

Presidents need to understand that a critical factor for success in the co-leadership model is that *co-leaders need a champion who allows him or her to succeed*. This success often includes an ability for the co-leader to subordinate his or her ego to attain a common goal—something both parties probably need. Each has to have a healthy ego, but these can't be perceived to clash. And presidents need to understand what type of co-leader they have.

In their research on the topic, Heenan and Bennis (1999, 11) believe that there are three main categories of successful co-leaders: crusaders, confederates, and consorts. Crusaders tend to be comfortable in serving a noble cause and believe in it passionately. Confederates tend to be comfortable in serving an exceptional organization or enterprise. Consorts, on the other hand, are those who serve an extraordinary person. Any one of these attributes can be valuable in a provost and make a contribution to the institution. In universities there are always more than enough *causes* to go around, and different people can fill the roles of crusader, confederate, or consort as desired. In selecting a provost, a president would be wise to probe the motivation of various candidates, seeking a co-leader who balances the president's own causes and is a good match with the needs of the institution and the talents of other members of the leadership team.

Another best practice involves *understanding the importance of presidential support for the provost personally*. Those in positions of responsibility know that "it is lonely at the top," and the president may be the only person a provost can talk to regularly about organizational or sometimes personal matters. In an open relationship the provost can complain about other vice presidents, discuss the strengths and weaknesses of deans, express frustration with the faculty even as he supports their efforts, and perhaps even complain about the impatience of the board of trustees. The president is often the only one to whom such comments can be made with the complete assurance that they will not be repeated outside the room.

Presidents also need to make sure that provosts take care of their personal time. Provosts need to be encouraged to take vacations, conserve their energy for the important issues, and make sure they're dealing with the right issues. Again, perhaps the only one in the organization concerned about the provost's personal development will be the president. And excellent provosts will understand the importance of having the same concerns for the president's personal well-being.

Presidents will benefit from understanding and, if possible, supporting the career aspirations of their provosts. The professional development of provosts is not a common topic in the literature of higher education. To what does a provost aspire—a presidency, remaining as a provost, retirement, or returning to the faculty? Heenan and Bennis (1999, 9–10) point out that, because all leadership is situational, it is difficult to categorize co-leaders. But in the course of their research they found three distinctive career paths: fast-trackers, back-trackers, and on-trackers.

Fast-trackers are those who are on the way up. Many of them aspire to be presidents in their own right, and the current job is primarily a rite of passage. And indeed, being a provost is a time-honored path to the presidency, although this career route is becoming more complex in the modern university. Fast-trackers tend to be good at "building their own cadre of talented lieutenants," and they often understand "in the most visceral of ways the value of sharing power" (Heenan and Bennis 1999, 9).

Back-trackers may be people who are former presidents or have down-shifted their aspirations. They tend not to be interested in the pressure of the number one job and want to avoid the nerve rattling and revolving-door syndrome of today's presidencies. They are typified by the person who finds "greater peace in being the quiet power behind the throne" (Heenan and Bennis 1999, 10).

On-trackers are those who either didn't or don't want a presidency or weren't promoted into it. Heenan and Bennis (1999, 10) report that the on-trackers are "comfortable remaining as part of a vibrant team of leaders," although they would accept top jobs or top billings if offered. The key is that they "find ways to prosper as supporting players."

The president must understand whether he has a fast-tracker, back-tracker, or on-tracker as a provost. In the case of fast-trackers, the president has to decide whether he wishes to help or hinder the aspirations of the provost to become a president, maybe even to take his/her job. If the decision is that the provost is not ready to move up, tensions will develop between the president and the provost over the provost's professional goals.

If the president is supportive of the fast-tracker's aspirations, a balance will need to be struck so that current responsibilities can be aligned with these longer-range aspirations. For example, it is difficult to maintain a co-leadership focus and direction if the provost comes to be perceived as a "short-timer" who can't wait to get on to his/her real goal. It can be disastrous if the provost is perceived to want to replace a current president not ready to move on. Presidential support for back-trackers and on-trackers is, first and foremost, to respect and honor the role they have chosen and ensure that they have opportunities *to shine* at what they do best.

Like all good leaders, *presidents and provosts need to listen.* It is part of the human condition to make it difficult for others to tell us what we don't want to hear. Presidents and provosts are particularly prone to this human frailty. They live in something of a rarified and isolated environment and often are at or near the pinnacle of their careers. Many (not all) have achieved these positions because they are competent and skilled professionals; they pride themselves on being good listeners. Such leaders often do not appreciate how difficult it is for even their most trusted advisers to share tough messages with them. We speak here not of the many who are always willing to tell university leaders "what they think" and usually do so in public settings. Rather, we speak of those who, with the leader's and institution's best interest at heart, are willing in private, quiet times to risk sharing observations that they know the boss does not want to hear. To accept advice given by such individuals without annoyance, animosity, or retribution, even if the leader is absolutely certain that the advice cannot be acted on, is a special skill that can open avenues of information not usually available to presidents. And to do so in a way that the bearer of the tidings may again risk "telling me what I don't want to hear" is an art form.

And finally, to buttress the role of the provost, the president should *organize efforts to demonstrate that the provost is influential and a major factor in the leadership of the institution.* Whether this is serving as acting president when the president is out of town, presiding at various ceremonies, or leading and effectively deciding major actions will depend on the culture of the institution. Nevertheless, it is one of the major responsibilities of the president to ensure that the provost is perceived to be influential in university affairs. It is becoming apparent in American higher education that the development of a "leadership team" is paramount to a president's success and that of the institution. There is no more important member of that team than the provost, so the issue becomes how these two leaders can work together successfully to accomplish leadership team goals.

SUMMARY

This chapter began with a description of the roles of the president and the provost. Although presidents believe academic affairs to be one of their most troublesome issue areas, they spend most of their time on other activities. The provost is crucial in effectively pursuing an institution's academic agenda and as such in providing leadership in an area a president deems important but to which he or she may not be able to give adequate attention. Unfortunately, it is often the case that presidents and provosts do not serve together long enough to develop the effective working relationship needed to support each other when dealing with complex academic matters. The Mythical State case and several others illustrate the difficulties that can ensue when these co-leaders do not serve together for extended periods of time, represent different stakeholders, or have conflicting strategies to effect change. This chapter went on to discuss elements and best practices involved in developing effective co-leadership working relationships between presidents and provosts.

In Chapter 6 we turn to a discussion of the big issue of strategic planning, focusing on it from the perspective of governance and what it can tell us about participation claims, decision making, and lessons learned.

CHAPTER 6

The Governance of Strategic Planning

You've got to be careful if you don't know where you're going because you might not get there.

—Yogi Berra, *The Yogi Book*

On a sunny spring afternoon, the vice president for institutional planning was sitting at his desk considering the task that the president of only two months had just passed on. Earlier in the day the president had stopped by his office and said in a casual but serious manner, "I need a new strategic plan and I can't wait for a year before one is completed." The vice president was not overjoyed at the prospect of coordinating the development of yet another strategic plan, but he did not find the president's directive surprising. He had worked for several presidents and realized that, early in their tenure, each new president directed the preparation of a new or revised plan for the university. To reduce the chances of a planning process that "might not get there," the vice president decided to review previous planning efforts for lessons learned.

In this chapter, the vice president's assignment provides a setting for considering the art form involved in the governance of strategic planning. To give the analysis a context, we use the case of four strategic planning processes undertaken by a higher education system over more than 20 years. We analyze these efforts by focusing on how various *claims for participation* unfold. The chapter concludes with lessons that might assist senior planning officers and institutions in general when undertaking a cycle of strategic planning.

STATE UNIVERSITY

Background

More than 30 years ago, State University (State U) expanded into a system of heterogeneous campuses, a feature that sets it apart from a system of institutions with similar missions. State U enrolls more than 50,000 students and includes a dominant doctoral/research campus, two largely baccalaureate campuses, and a number of open-door community colleges.

In the early years of the State U system, the governing board and president prepared two seminal planning documents that translated the institution's statutory purposes into its mission: the discovery, examination, preservation, and transmission of knowledge, wisdom, and values; access for qualified residents; and open-door access at two-year campuses. Over the years, this mission language was carried forward in planning documents and board policies and was eventually incorporated into formal system and campus mission statements.

For a period spanning nine presidencies, State U prepared numerous academic plans. In the early years these plans encompassed all parts of the system. As the system grew, however, they were prepared separately for each campus and became known as strategic plans. State U also engaged in facility planning with documents that were prepared by external consultants; these plans mapped existing and planned facilities and formed the basis for capital budget requests.

System Academic/Strategic Plans

Over 20-plus years, State U completed four major academic plans, designated either as master or strategic plans. Although the development of all four State U plans involved all institutional constituents, including students, this case focuses on the relationships among the board, administrators, and faculty in these planning processes. We are interested in what can be learned from this case about each of these parties' legitimate governance claims and how their claims were met. Table 6.1 provides a synopsis of plan participants and components.

Plan 1

The university president is credited with initiating the concept that resulted in the university's first strategic plan. The system vice president for academic affairs (VPAA) and the chief planning officer (CPO) were key leaders of the planning process; the board provided overall commitment and support. A strategic plan steering committee, appointed by the president, consisted of three faculty senate leaders, one faculty intern, five campus administrators, the system VPAA who served as chair, and the CPO who coordinated the work of the committee. In response to an open invitation to the university community, approximately 200 faculty and staff from throughout the system participated in a strategic planning colloquium and multiple task forces. Drawing on task force reports, the plan was drafted under the overall guidance of the steering committee, with the CPO handling the writing and document preparation tasks.

Table 6.1
State University: Synopsis of Four Academic Plan Processes

	Plan 1	Plan 2	Plan 3	Plan 4
Board role	• Overall support and commitment	• Initiate plan development and hire consultant	• Advice and comment	• Review
	• Review	• Review	• Review	• Plan approval
	• Plan approval	• Plan approval	• Plan approval	
Faculty role	• Members of steering committee	• Subject of interviews and consultation sessions	• Comment and provide feedback on drafts	• Serve on steering committee
	• Serve on task forces	• Comment on drafts	• Subject of consultation session	• Participate in workshop
	• Participate in colloquium			• Serve on issue teams
	• Comment on drafts			• Comment on drafts
President's role	• Initiate plan development	• Subject of interviews	• Initiate plan development	• Initiate plan development
	• Active in using the plan to make the university's case		• Active in using the plan to advance strategic directions	• Conduct forums during plan development
Administration's role	• Coordinate process	• Subject of interviews	• Coordinate planning process	• Coordinate planning process
	• Draft plan		• Draft plan	• Draft plan
Student role	• Serve on task forces	• Subject of interviews	• Subject of briefings	• Serve on steering committee
	• Opportunity to comment	• Opportunity to comment	• Opportunity to comment	• Participate in workshop and on issue teams
				• Opportunity to comment

(Continued)

Table 6.1
State University: Synopsis of Four Academic Plan Processes (*Continued*)

	Plan 1	Plan 2	Plan 3	Plan 4
Preparation time	@ 12 months	@ 13 months	@ 12 months	@ 12 months

Plan components	• Preamble/ mission and components of the system
	
	• Planning assumptions
	
	• Major themes/ strategic dimensions
	
	  – Objectives
	
	  – Priority actions
		• University setting
		
		• Major goals
		
		  – Activities to achieve goals
		
		  – Recommendations
			• Companion document
			
			  – Mission
			
			  – Vision
			
			  – Common values
			
			  – System description
			
			• Planning context
			
			• Planning assumptions
			
			• Major goals
			
			  – Planning principles
			
			  – Action strategies
				• Vision
				
				• Mission statement
				
				• Commitments
				
				• Core values
				
				• Evolution of the system
				
				• Planning imperatives
				
				• Major goals
				
				  – Objectives
				
				  – Action strategies

Role of consultants	• None	• Prepare the plan	• None	• Advice and consultation

Plan preparation spanned an academic year. The administration was committed to presenting the plan to the board in June. Most faculty received copies of the draft plan about May 15; two days later the faculty congress at the research campus met and discussed the plan with the acting president and the chief planning officer. On June 14, the senate executive committee from the research campus wrote to the acting president that the plan had not been acted on by that campus's faculty congress, senate, or executive committee; the plan had serious shortcomings; the process thus far had failed to provide opportunity for serious faculty consideration; and the senate was ready to assist in the review and revision in accordance with mutually agreed procedures. On this same date, a revised version of the plan had been transmitted to the board for a June 21 consultation session. Shortly thereafter the acting president met with the research campus senate executive committee and also shared in writing that, although the planning timeframe may not have provided as much time for deliberation as desirable, it was not necessary to again refer the plan to this senate because it was a systemwide document and not a campus plan. The board adopted the plan in July.

Plan 2

The major issue that prompted State U's next round of planning was the need for an expanded university presence in two underserved regions of the state. The legislature supported this effort by providing funds to develop a 10-year State U master plan. The board retained the services of two consultants (retired, highly respected members of the university community) to develop the master plan. Their work spanned approximately 13 months and culminated in board adoption of a master plan. This plan was intended to serve as a planning guide for the growth of the university for a decade.

The process used for the development of this master plan included (1) consultant interviews and meetings with faculty, staff, and students at all campuses of the system; (2) analysis of university, state, and national data; (3) extensive examination of recent studies in the field; (4) comprehensive introspection by the consultants; and (5) public meetings at which administrators, students, and faculty were provided the opportunity to address the recommendations contained in the plan. The consultants wrote the plan.

Shortly after adopting the master plan, the board instructed the administration to quickly prepare an implementation plan and the system planning office was so charged. Given the short turnaround time allowed, the faculty role in the development of the implementation plan was limited. Two months after adopting the master plan, the board approved the implementation plan with the understanding that specific actions would require approval in accordance with established board policies and procedures.

As part of the implementation process, it was recognized that the university needed to engage in "mission maintenance." State U had undergone considerable change since adoption of the institution's earlier mission statement. The roles of the separate campuses within the system needed clarity. Draft documents drew on the earlier mission statement and relevant language from campus academic plans. When a change in presidential leadership occurred, work on campus mission statements was put on hold pending the appointment of a permanent president.

Plan 3

A new president took office approximately two years after the board adopted plan 2, and he quickly concluded that changes in State U's environment required a new plan. The institution was facing budget cuts and competition for scarce state dollars. Internally, enrollments were up; the impact of information technology was pervasive and profound; federal funds were increasing; and there were more accountability, regulation, and oversight demands. State U campuses were behaving more as a system, but all had serious infrastructure shortfalls and needed to establish priorities and make choices. This president wanted a planning document that facilitated priority setting.

Preparation of plan 3 took approximately 12 months from start to the time of board approval, but spanned parts of two academic years:

1. Senior officers prepared an initial draft that drew on their priority-setting activities. The president charged a system academic affairs council, comprised of campus academic affairs staff and the system CPO, to take lead responsibility for managing the planning effort.

2. A draft plan was broadly distributed, and comments and input were solicited from the board, campus administrators, faculty senates, student governments, collective bargaining units, legislators, and business leaders.

3. A period of review and consultation involving multiple campus meetings spanned four months.

4. The administration inventoried all comments and used this input to revise the plan.

5. A second draft plan was distributed to the university's internal and external communities; the board was briefed on the status of the process and its guidance sought on the substance of the plan.

6. Another round of consultation took place, affording faculty, students, administrators, and external constituents the opportunity to comment on the draft plan; forums were held for students and the public.

7. Based on this round of consultation, the plan was again revised and, along with updated mission statements, it was adopted by the board. Subsequently, separate campus strategic plans were developed and adopted by the board, and board and executive policies directing the periodic updating of mission statements and system and campus strategic plans were adopted.

The mission update effort that had begun several years earlier proceeded at the same time, but separately from the development of plan 3. Earlier draft mission statements were refined, broadly distributed for comments, shared at public forums, revised, and approved by the board. The mission of State U now recognized common system values and separate missions by campus type (research, four-, and two-year campuses).

Plan 4

A new president took office approximately four-and-a-half years after board adoption of plan 3. He quickly determined that he wanted an updated strategic plan that would guide his administration's priorities over the next eight years. The VPAA was charged with lead responsibility, and the system planning office and academic affairs council staffed the overall effort. Partway through the effort, a consultant assisted with organizing the process and preparing templates for work products.

This planning process spanned an academic year:

1. The academic affairs council and faculty senate chairs solicited from the senates and other system groups cross-cutting issues that would form the basis for imperatives guiding State U's future service to the state and beyond.

2. Several faculty senate chairs and the system academic affairs council were appointed as the steering committee.

3. Using the results of the issue exercise, the steering committee drafted strategic directions and planned a system workshop.

4. A mid-year workshop of approximately 300 faculty, staff, administrators, students, and public leaders used the strategic directions to draft strategic goals and action strategies.

5. At midyear, a president's advisory council on plans and priorities was appointed; its membership included students, faculty, administrators, and staff. Over time, additional administrators were added to this body. This council guided the remaining stages of plan development, assisted with draft preparation, vetted draft documents, and participated in a final planning retreat.

6. The president and the vice president for academic affairs held several forums/roundtables with students, alumni, and business, union, and government leaders.

7. Results of the system workshop were refined by the planning office and grouped into goals; each goal was assigned to a strategic issue team. These teams had approximately 15 members drawn from different campuses and university constituents (faculty, students, and administrators/staff). Teams refined assigned goals, developed action strategies, and submitted a report to the council.

8. The council assisted the planning office with assembling a draft strategic plan that was distributed electronically to the State U community.

9. Approximately 100 comments were received and inventoried. Using electronic mail, the planning office kept the planning council and university community informed about revisions that were made and those suggestions that were not used.

10. A revised plan was shared with the board for consultation and placed on line. Feedback resulted in additional revisions and board approval.

Analysis of Legitimacy Claims and the Decision-Making Process

The Board

The board's claim and authority to approve all four plans was undisputed. The action taken was *approval in principle*. This meant that specific proposals cited in the plans were subject to the board's usual program, budget, organization, and related approval processes. The board was active in advocating the creation of mission statements that were developed separately from plan 3.

Before acting on plan 1, the board's involvement consisted of overall commitment and support throughout the planning process. The board had considerable involvement with the development of plan 2 by virtue of the fact that it initiated the plan's development and hired the consultants who prepared it. The board commented and provided advice on the planning process and the substance of plan 3 and willingly contributed side-bar statements included in the final document. The board was instrumental in directing the administration to share the last major draft of this plan with a large and varied number of external community groups. In the case of plan 4, the board's role was primarily one of review of the final document.

For all four plans, the board relied on the administration or, in the case of plan 2, the consultants, to prepare the substance of each plan. The board exercised its claim to review and make suggestions about topics that might be expanded on, but in general it refrained from directing the substance of the plans. And for all four plans, the board sought assurances that the university community, including faculty, staff, and students, had the opportunity to be consulted as the plans were developed.

As each of the four planning processes was coming to closure, the board pursued the issue of how the plan would be funded. They expressed this claim for involvement by asking, "Where would the cash come from?" To this end, the administration responded with activities that included developing detailed agendas for action, implementation plans, and, with varying degrees of success, the construction of biennium budget requests that reflected plan goals and objectives.

The Administration

The administration typically exercised the claim to initiate, staff, draft, and bring a final plan forward for board approval. The university president initiated the strategic plan processes for plans 1, 3, and 4. The president retired shortly before the board acted to adopt plan 1, and the vice president for academic affairs was appointed president within the next year. As vice president, he and his staff had played a key role in plan development. The claims raised at the end of the process by the dominant campus senate subsided in part because of his ongoing dialogue with that body.

The system planning office actively coordinated the preparation of plans 1, 3, and 4 by facilitating the planning process, preparing background data and analyses, and handling the drafting and preparation of documents. In the case of plan 2, the primary role of the president and university administrators was as subjects of interviews and participants in consultation sessions. At the consultants' request the administration prepared a variety of data displays and analyses.

The process that was used to prepare plans 1, 3, and 4, but especially plan 3, assumed a claim for legitimate participation by the university's senior officers who would be expected to implement the plan. The initial drafts of plan 3 were prepared by the administration, and senior officers were actively involved in deciding how to incorporate the comments and advice forwarded by members of the university community. In the case of plan 4, the gradual expansion of the president's planning council to include more and more administrators provides evidence of a claim for involvement by those who anticipate responsibility for dealing with the concerns raised in plans and securing the funding needed to implement plans.

The Faculty

In addition to having several members serve on the steering committee for plan 1, the faculty were speakers at the colloquium that kicked off the planning effort and served as members or chairs of seven task forces. In this latter capacity, faculty played key roles in drafting task force reports; these reports informed the final plan document. Despite this level of participation, the dominant campus's faculty senate maintained that their legitimate claim for "serious faculty consideration" of the plan was not met. Further, the acting president was informed by this senate that the senate expected to review and act on the final plan—an opportunity they did not have. The acting president took the position that it was not necessary to refer the plan to this senate for such action because the plan was a system and not a campus plan.

The role of faculty in the development of plan 2 was primarily as the subject of interviews and as participants in consultation and document review sessions with the consultants. Faculty, through their senates or as individuals, were afforded the opportunity to comment in detail on all aspects of the drafts of plan 3. The comments of those who chose to participate were compiled and, by decision of the university's senior officers, used to modify the plan as appropriate. However, no real mechanism, other than the next draft of the plan, was used to convey back to the faculty how their input had influenced plan development. Although not evident through complaints or concerns raised at the time, this lack of a feedback mechanism and the resulting perception that this plan was developed through a top-down process proved to be a source of complaint aired by some faculty from the research campus to the regional accrediting team visiting the campus several years later.

In the preparation of plan 4, faculty participated in a system workshop, served on the steering committee and issue teams, assisted with draft language, and commented on draft documents. The use of the Internet to post procedures and documents, list participants, receive comments, and (probably most important) to post exactly how comments were used, modified, or not used for each new draft of the plan set this effort apart from processes used for earlier plans.

CASE DYNAMICS AND SAVVY PLANNERS

Returning to the task before the CPO with which we opened this chapter, we observe that a number of lessons can be learned from the State U case and our analysis of participatory claims. These lessons are not prescriptions or guarantees for successful strategic planning. Every institution is different, and lessons about planning processes and implementation must be tailored to institutional circumstances (helpful references include Harvey 2003, 234; Shulock and Harrison 2003, 137; and Rowley and Sherman 2003). What follows is a set of observations, drawn from one statewide system of higher education's experience with planning. The focus is on common sense and politically savvy behavior.

Establish Priorities and Honor All

Insist that plans contain priorities while honoring the work of all. It is difficult to design and manage a strategic planning process that results in a plan that sets clear priorities and also has broad buy-in. A common characteristic of institutional strategic plans is that they include something for everyone; they are "kitchen sink" documents. By including a large number of objectives, they try to be all things to all people (Shulock and Harrison 2003, 138). As a result, such documents help guide decision making only in the broadest sense. For better or worse, the broad nature of the goals in the State U plans suggests that they fit this pattern.

In considering the development of the four strategic plans at State U over a period that spanned five presidencies and more than 20 years and involved both top-down and bottom-up efforts, we found that there tends to be an inverse relationship between the support/buy-in/ownership that can be mustered for a system strategic plan and the existence of specific priorities in that plan. Faculty look to strategic plans to provide *windows of opportunity* that will advance agendas in which they are invested. In some instances presidents are hesitant to endorse plans with specific priorities. They perceive that such priorities will limit their capacity to pursue whatever seems desirable or expedient at the time. And presidents and other executives may be concerned that defined priorities will be used to hold them accountable for accomplishments they perceive to be beyond their capacity to deliver. Moore (2003, 13) noted this concern as "fear that unsophisticated planners and their planning processes will get in the way of presidential leadership by prematurely conveying strategic initiatives or limiting presidential options." This limitation on flexibility was reflected in presidential opposition to the planning council's effort to establish explicit priorities as the plan 4 process was drawing to a close.

When these two forces combine—faculty from numerous disciplines arguing that their areas of endeavor must have visibility and be accommodated in the plan, and executives uncomfortable with defined priorities—it should not come as a surprise that the resulting compromise language can be perceived as a motherhood-and-apple-pie outcome. Table 6.2 summarizes the major goals/objectives of the four State U plans and demonstrates that, despite changes in board membership, presidents, faculty leaders, and the environment, the goals of these plans fall into common categories: (1) achieving quality/excellence/effectiveness/student success, (2) serving the state/providing access/functioning as a system, (3) championing diversity, (4) advancing the institution's comparative advantage, and (5) acquiring and exercising stewardship over resources.

In general, we found that the more detailed and refined the priorities of a plan, the narrower the support base for that plan. Even plan 3, which generally had broad language but broke new ground by naming seven core colleges as priorities, drew criticism from the colleges not listed. These colleges/schools perceived that they were "left out," and some support from them could only be mustered by ensuring that other parts of the plan made reference to the importance of their programs.

Table 6.2
State University: Academic Plan Goals/Objectives

Plan 1	Plan 2	Plan 3	Plan 4
Achieving program quality	Striving for excellence in undergraduate education and continuing to gain prominence in research	Providing access to quality educational experiences	Educational effectiveness and student success
Serving the state	Revitalizing service to the state	Providing service to the state	A learning, research, and service network
	Expanding access to educational opportunity throughout the state	Implementing differentiated campus missions and functioning as a system	
Enhancing the essence of a university	Maintaining diversity by clarifying campus missions and coordinating campus plans	Continuing to champion diversity and respect for differences	Investment in faculty, staff, students, and their environment
Establishing an international and comparative advantage focus	Enhancing the international role of the university	Strengthening the university as a premier resource in areas of unique and comparative strength and advancing its international role	A model local, regional, and global university
Adapting to scientific and technological change	Improving the organization, financing, and image of the university	Acquiring resources and managing them with accountability and responsiveness	Resources and stewardship

A lesson learned is that one of the most difficult leadership issues in universities and colleges is that of establishing priorities while still providing support and conveying appreciation for the work of a broad spectrum of professionals. It is difficult for a president to send the message, and even more difficult for faculty to receive the message, that an area of endeavor in which they are invested is a lower priority than another area of work. It takes a great deal of political savvy on the part of institutional leaders to achieve a strategic plan with a defined set of priorities that will direct the future of the institution and achieve this outcome while garnering broad-based internal support for the plan. Institutional leaders and presidents in particular must find ways to speak publicly about the importance and need for priorities while also honoring the important work of all. In the case of plan 3, the president attempted to send this message by speaking regularly of the need to *achieve and maintain quality across the board* while identifying and focusing on *areas in which the institution could be exceptionally strong.*

Broad Participation and Timely Decision Making

Understand that broad-based participation in the planning effort takes time; don't expect a new strategic plan to help with major short-term decisions. One of the real challenges in managing any strategic planning process is dealing with the tension between achieving broad participation and completing the plan within the timeframe needed for decision making. Each of the State U plans took approximately one year to complete. This is not unusual. Shulock and Harrison (2003, 139) note that the strategic plan for California State University-Sacramento took three years to complete.

The stages of strategic planning are well documented (Cope 1981; Kotler and Murphy 1981; Keller 1983; Shirley 1988). A brief summary of typical strategic planning steps makes the case that, even when done expeditiously, it takes a lengthy period of time to: (1) review and possibly revise the current core elements of the organization (mission, clientele served, program mix, comparative advantage, and other assets); (2) assess external conditions (opportunities and threats); (3) match these external realities against internal capacities (strengths and weaknesses); and (4) develop strategic directions intended to reaffirm or bring about change in the institution's core elements.

Claims for involvement in these strategic planning activities are many and broad-based, going well beyond elected faculty leaders. A plan for a higher education system will encompass at least the following claims: faculty leaders who may or may not be part of senates, faculty program/department heads, campus administrators, deans, professional and blue collar staff, students, alumni, and business and government leaders. Typically, the plans produced as a result of these participatory claims are general in nature and expected to span a multiyear timeframe. Presidents faced with major unanticipated budget cuts (as was the State U case in the mid 1990s) do not find it helpful to have to wait a year for a strategic plan that in the end may not have the priorities needed to manage budget cuts that arrive on very short notice.

Plan 3 attempted to deal at least in part with this difficulty by "front-loading" the process. Instead of appointing a committee and working a broad-based "bottom-up" process that would provide a draft plan in six months or more, the administration pulled together relevant existing documents and quickly prepared a draft document. Then the process was "back-loaded" with an extensive time for feedback and consultation that refined the plan. This process had the advantage of providing the president with basic planning principles that could be used in upcoming budget consultations with the board and the state. It had the disadvantage, expressed after the plan was completed, that the plan was developed in too much of a top-down mode.

In the plan 1 instance, the goal on the part of the administration and board to complete the plan by about the end of an academic year meant that the drafting and document review stages were collapsed. Despite what had been an inclusive and lengthy process, this timely completion goal was perceived as limiting the faculty's legitimate claim for participation.

If we accept the time-consuming nature of broad-scale involvement in strategic planning and that the resulting plan, albeit general in nature, is necessary, we conclude that strategic plans are not sufficient planning/decision tools to deal with unexpected budget cuts or opportunities. Events that institutions must deal with generally cannot wait for a new strategic plan that directs the shape of the next budget. A difficult but important responsibility of the vice president, whose assignment opened this chapter, is to advise the president that developing a new strategic plan with a substantive faculty role will take at least a year and to suggest to the president a shorter-term agenda/priority setting strategy. We will return to this lesson as we discuss the value of agenda setting.

Faculty Participation and Influence

Make the distinction early in the process between faculty influence on plan substance and faculty approval of plans. In the case of plan 1, the extensive involvement of faculty in the development process was not in the end sufficient to satisfy the dominant senate's expectation that its claim for legitimate participation required that it review and *act* on the final plan. There appeared to be agreement between the administration and faculty regarding the legitimacy of the faculty's participation and influence up to the point of acting on the final plan. At that final stage, expectations diverged.

Several lessons emerge. Not providing adequate time for review of a final draft may invite unreasonable expectations with regard to who approves the plan. The end of the process is not the ideal time to differentiate faculty influence from faculty action. Also, fairness is always an issue when dealing with multiple senates within a system. The senate from a dominant campus is not one among equals in terms of plan influence, but its influence does not necessarily extend to unilateral action on a system plan. Working out these understandings early in the process should facilitate the end game.

If faculty are unaware of their influence in plan development, they could well perceive that they have none—process is critical in this regard. A difficult lesson emerged from the preparation of plan 3. In this case, it wasn't enough to give faculty the opportunity to comment on multiple plan drafts and methodically incorporate their feedback into future drafts. Faculty must perceive that this is happening, and this requires the capacity to communicate directly with faculty in a timely manner. The administration's detailed inventory of all input and the resulting changes to drafts of plan 3 were not apparent to the faculty. The lack of a steering committee with faculty membership added to the perception that the faculty voice had not been central to plan development. The perception that faculty are involved is as important—and in some cases may be more important—than actually influencing plan substance.

Technology—A Valuable Aid to Transparency

Use technology, no matter how time-consuming, to communicate the manner in which constituent comments have influenced plan substance. Technologies in the form of e-mail and word processing have added transparency to strategic planning processes. The capacity to communicate with nearly every member of a system of campuses has dramatically changed consultation processes associated with the development of major institutional plans and policies. The use of electronic communications at State U was considerably more sophisticated during the preparation of plan 4 than earlier. The university community was blanketed with routine updates and multiple drafts that highlighted and made it easy for faculty, students, and others to see changes made from earlier drafts. These highlighted versions of documents, plus summary transmittals, proved to be worth the considerable effort it took to prepare them. They made it possible for the very small share of the university community who had submitted comments and revisions to understand how their ideas had been used or not used. It also made it possible for faculty to communicate more easily with each other and the steering committee. And it sent a message to the silent but observant faculty majority that the faculty voice was being heard. A lesson that emerged is that most faculty do not tend to get directly involved in the time-consuming processes associated with strategic planning, but they want to know that faculty who are involved are given a voice and taken seriously.

Line Officers and Faculty—The Delivery Folks

Be sure that those expected to lead implementation of plan priorities, especially priorities with resource implications, are "in the room" as the plan is developed. The four State U plans reinforced the principle that strategic planning processes must involve both faculty *and* line officers. To ensure broad participation in strategic planning, it is common practice to appoint and charge a strategic plan steering committee that includes representatives of institutional constituents (see Schuster et al. 1994). Plans 1 and 4 benefited from the existence of such a body. Plan 3 had considerable involvement of line officers, but it lacked the visible involvement of faculty on a steering committee. This, along with the lack of transparency, resulted in the interesting phenomenon of a plan that drew no substantive criticism but was perceived to be the result of a less than ideal process. Swenk (1999) describes a case in which the failure to include program faculty directly affected by the planning for a school was a significant factor in delaying the creation of this school for nearly a decade. In all of these cases the lesson learned is that process matters.

Plan 2 relied heavily on the work of consultants, with limited roles for both the administration and faculty. As a result, line institutional administrators who were expected to find the resources to implement the plan and deliver results lacked the involvement and personal investment needed to make the plan work. A reasonable planning document can collect dust on the shelf if executive officers see little relationship between the performance expected of them and "that plan." Keller (1983, 141) has observed that "unless the chief operating officers subscribe—or at least feel they cannot ignore or torpedo the strategy—the plan will not sail."

Partway through the development of plan 4, a steering committee was appointed that was broadly representative of the university community. In general, this process emphasized faculty participation. But it is instructive to note that, as the process moved forward, a realization unfolded that additional administrators needed to be added to the steering committee. In the last several critical meetings of this body, administrators outnumbered the faculty by a ratio of three to one. In summary, the lesson from the State U experience is that the line officers who will be expected to implement the plan have to be "in the room" and actively participate in plan development.

Plan Implementation Starts with Presidents

Don't underestimate the value of presidential repetition and cheerleading for the goals of a plan. There is an extensive literature that considers whether strategic plans make a difference, and much of it is summarized by Birnbaum (2000, 63–89) in his treatment of "Strategic Planning: The Grand Name Without the Grand Thing." Some have made the case that few plans produce transformational change but rather impact change on the margins, with the primary benefit resulting from the planning process rather than the substance of the plan (Harvey 2003, 233).

Based on the State U experience, we make the observation that strategic directions, broad though they may be, can make a difference when used by politically savvy presidents who understand the value of repeating these directions and using them at critical decision points. For example, repetition of strategic plan goals to legislators and other external constituents makes the case that "the university has its act together." Repetition of strategic plan goals internally enables astute presidents to lay the foundation for linking specific budget requests, major initiatives, and even reallocation decisions to these goals.

Plan 1 was used effectively by the newly appointed president to send the message to internal and external communities that State U had a plan for its future. This plan is generally credited with laying the foundation and garnering support for the establishment of two major schools at the research campus. This plan also set State U on a course to take advantage of emerging technologies.

Plan 3 benefited from a president who understood the value of repeating goals and constantly encouraging senior officers to make use of these goals in their operational and budgeting decisions. At weekly senior staff meetings, this president regularly found an opportunity to query, perhaps appear to test, those in the room about the goals of State U's strategic plan. In so doing he repeatedly sent the message that strategic goals were to be taken seriously and that he expected them to be incorporated in campus/college/school plans and to be translated into outcomes. He understood that, in the absence of such efforts, the accumulation of day-to-day decisions, especially budget decisions, becomes the plan. Strategic directions will not drive the long-term development of an institution if the day-to-day budget acquisition and allocation processes do not conform to those directions.

For example, if an institutional strategic plan sets forth the vision of a regional campus with limited graduate programs, but the campus pursues a pattern of funding on a par with a research campus, it could be argued that the institution's "real" strategic planning direction is to become a research institution. It takes constant attention to strategic goals to slow this form of "mission creep."

In the case of plan 3, the president's continuing attention to the system goal that addressed the importance of new revenue sources was translated into a strategy in the research campus's plan to offer incentives to professional schools to generate increased tuition and fees as a mechanism for underwriting their educational costs. Implementation of this strategy is generally credited with stabilizing the finances and future of State U's law school and garnering the resources much needed by the medical, nursing, and business schools.

Continuity across Plans Is Not a Bad Thing

Realize from the outset that the goals of a new plan will likely resemble those of the last plan; undertake the process for other reasons, so that valuable time and energy are not devoted to producing a repetitive result with little gain in other areas. Boards, faculty, and administrators who share in the governance of strategic planning with the expectation that it leads to a better managed institution could advance this cause by giving greater attention to planning continuity and agenda setting. It is time to recognize that the lack of continuity in the management of public higher education systems results, among other negatives, in time-consuming and redundant planning (Schmidtlein and Milton 1988–89). If there was a time when state systems could afford to use scarce resources for this purpose, the competitive environment in which public higher education now finds itself suggests that such a time is past.

It is a given that presidential leadership of strategic planning is key to its success. And some new and long-serving presidents will need updated plans. The incorporation of mission and plan-maintenance requirements in State U board policy recognized this reality. Unfortunately, the lack of continuity in presidential leadership can mean that, whether needed or not, a new, costly strategic planning effort is undertaken with every new presidential appointment and sometimes as a tool to encourage a sitting president to move on. In the State U case, it is noteworthy that the president was not asked by the board to lead the preparation of plan 2 and that plan 1, for which he had provided key leadership, had not run its course. This sent a signal that a change in leadership was afoot; the president announced his resignation approximately one year after the board acted on plan 2.

Presidential searches often seek candidates who have very different strengths from their predecessors. New presidents are installed with a general understanding that they are to provide a different style of leadership from that of the presidents they followed. It should not come as a surprise that new presidents who find themselves in this situation move as quickly as they deem acceptable to replace the existing institutional planning document, no matter what its usefulness, with one of "their" own. A new planning cycle goes forward, and approximately a year later another plan is presented for adoption. This new plan often contains a set of goals that are similar to those of earlier plans. It may be that governing boards need to be more precise about their expectations. Boards need to distinguish between their desire for a change in presidential leadership style and their expectation that a president undertake planning that changes long-term institutional directions.

In the State U case, four system planning documents that spanned the administrations of five presidents with quite different styles and involved different planning processes each contained similar strategic goals. As Table 6.2 illustrates, the language used to present plan goals changed over the years, but the heart of each plan was a repetition of basic directions. With the exception of the substance of an institution's special niche, the themes evident in these goals are not unique to State U. In a national survey of higher education institutions, Kaplan (2004, 198) found that the three most popular strategic plan objectives were academic quality, enrollment growth, and improved facilities and technology. This finding mirrors our own assessment after reviewing planning documents, especially statewide or system plans from a number of states. Birnbaum (2000, 75), in his treatment of strategic planning, observed that "many plans turned out to be quite similar." The case study findings of others revealed that in some instances the large strategic planning issues tend to be amorphous and consume lengthy periods of deliberation, resulting in "little to show for the effort" (Schuster et al. 1994, 184).

Each State U plan was envisioned as spanning roughly 10 years, but none was in place that long. On average, plans 1, 2, and 3 had lifespans of five to seven years from the time of board adoption to the time the next planning cycle was completed. Keeping in mind that each planning cycle took approximately one year, the effective life span of each plan was even shorter. The result is a lot of planning and weak implementation. This charge applies to State U, but we doubt that it is unique to this institution.

The lesson to be learned is that seeking a different style of presidential leadership should not automatically be equated with the need for a new, full-blown, time-consuming, and costly planning process. A decoupling of thinking about presidential style and institutional directions could yield some badly needed management continuity and time to focus on plan implementation.

Agendas—Another Route to Priority Setting

Before undertaking a new planning cycle, consider whether annual or biannual agenda setting will address the needs at hand. Advocacy for continuity does not negate the need for updated plans. Planning is never over. It is a given that strategic directions need to be revisited at least every 8 to 10 years or more often if unusual circumstances warrant. In the intervening years, however, planning that takes the form of annual or biannual agenda setting carried out within the framework of existing strategic plan goals could bring some stability to the planning process, continuity to institutional directions, and attention where it is needed—on implementation. And effective implementation for any planning process means linking planning with budgeting to achieve "resource priorities" (Shulock and Harrison 2003, 138). Senior executives should be expected to explain how proposed budgets reflect resource priorities. Agenda/priority setting can take place on an annual or biannual basis and should involve presidents, senior executives, key faculty senate leaders, and leaders of other university constituencies. Using the operative strategic plan goals, the objective would be to settle on those resource and program priorities that would focus joint efforts by these shared governance partners in pursuit of institutional goals.

The Knight Higher Education Collaborative (2002) expands the concept of agenda setting to involve public officials and institutional leaders in collaborations that advance the public purposes of the state. The accountability demands placed on higher education require that strategic plans place more emphasis on achieving public agenda outcomes. Too often institutions and states move ahead without a collaborative effort to develop a state higher education agenda. A recent initiative in Virginia is evidence that such collaborations can take place. In Virginia the coming together of an institution-driven agenda and a governor's higher education agenda resulted in legislation that grants the state's public institutions more power to conduct certain operations while holding them to performance goals targeted directly at state needs (Couturier 2006). The success of this joint effort will, of course, depend on its implementation.

OBSERVATIONS

"Planners are usually inclined toward logical processes and view institutional politics as introducing dysfunction into an organization that should be more rational" (Moore 2003, 16). In our experience, academics in general have a tendency to view the political model as an inappropriate way of thinking about higher education governance. This, despite the fact that "smash mouth" political behavior is often all too evident on some campuses.

As a participant in one of the premier professional development seminars for higher education executives offered by a prestigious Ivy League school, it was interesting to observe the cool reception the participants had to the analysis advanced by the speaker who elaborated on "the political frame" (Bolman and Deal 1997, 159–175). It was as if many in attendance knew that power, influence, bargaining, and negotiation were all part of their lives back home, but they did not want to regard the political mode as legitimate. The proposition that "it is not inevitable that power and politics are demeaning and destructive" (175) can be difficult to embrace by those brought up in an academic culture that values rationality above all.

We end this chapter with several observations, all of which derive from the principle that the art form involved in the governance of academic planning requires understandings grounded in knowledge of "the university" as a political setting.

First, planners and presidents must face reality—they are participants in a political process. Planners might prefer to view their role as the apolitical managers of the planning process. Moore (2003, 16–17) summarizes several maxims that illustrate why such a view is unrealistic.

- Planning is technical, but it has political dimensions.
- Planners exercise political influence when they do their job of filtering, summarizing, analyzing, shaping, and sharing information and data.
- Planners exercise power as they deal with people in power and assist with decision making.
- Planners influence decisions because they influence what issues are addressed, by whom, how, when, and in what arenas. In so doing they help to determine who gets what, when, and how much.

Second, politically savvy planners and presidents realize that planning that makes a difference usually involves reaching "agreement about difficult issues rooted in competing values" (Moore 2003, 16). And dealing with these "wicked problems," as they are referred to by Rittel and Webber (1973, 155), requires credible processes. Such planning processes ought to have at least the following characteristics:

- Presidential leadership, leadership of the senior officers, board commitment, and an empowered senior planner.
- Clarity about the purposes for undertaking the planning process, with a clear focus on the good of the total institution. This means listening to the concerns that justify the planning effort and articulating them for the university community in a manner that builds consensus for the task ahead.
- Faculty buy-in to the planning process.

Other characteristics of credible processes, especially applicable to planning, that will be discussed more fully in Chapter 7 include:

- Agreement on a timeframe that has an end. The purpose of the undertaking will help determine the length of the process, but all participants need to understand from the outset that there is a clock ticking.
- A process that is widely communicated.
- A process that gives faculty the opportunity to influence the substance of the plan.
- Feedback after each stage of the planning process.
- Up-front clarity about who will act on the plan.

Third, savvy planners, whether they are planning officers or provosts, have close working relationships with presidents but never "play president." The tasks associated with managing the planning process, gathering needed data and information, presenting findings, and communicating with institutional constituents and with the decision makers must be done with utmost discretion. It requires doing for a president what the president would do if he or she had more time, but doing it in such a fashion that all parties, including the president, view the positive final results as reflecting *presidential leadership*. The planner should expect to "to carry the water" for results that are viewed as less than ideal. That is simply the price a senior officer pays for being a senior officer.

At every stage, the planner must be perceived as giving the advocates on all sides of wicked problems the opportunity to make their case. Those who provide input must come away with the sense that their ideas were translated fairly and, if not used, it was not because the planning officer unilaterally decided to leave their concerns on the cutting room floor. Even when they do not like the result, university constituents generally understand that presidents have to make tough decisions; however, they will not be tolerant of planning officers who overstep their bounds.

And finally, an effective planning/priority-setting process is one of the most important venues in which administrators and faculty participate in shared governance. Together they share the governance of planning through joint participation in the development of the plan. Here it is important that faculty have the opportunity for involvement and perceive that their participation is taken seriously. Faculty leaders and administrators share the responsibility for establishing the resource priorities that will implement the plan. It is critical that faculty senates understand that the leaders they select will be expected to sit with senior executives, work within the framework of the goals of the strategic plan, and use available assessment and institutional research data and information for the purpose of identifying the resource priorities that will drive the budget-setting process.

This form of shared governance does not involve plebiscites or even faculty senate votes on annual or biannual budget priorities. It requires the identification by senates of politically savvy faculty leaders who will participate in establishing institutional, not personal, priorities. And it requires politically savvy presidents who value and mentor these faculty leaders, understanding that they may be the most valuable "administrators" on their team and will determine the fate of shared governance at their institutions.

SUMMARY

This chapter began by considering the charge to a CPO from a new president who felt strongly the need for a new strategic plan. We reviewed the academic planning experience of a state university system under many different presidents and focused particularly on four major strategic plans spanning more than 20 years. The analysis of these four plans showed that, although the planning processes varied, the plans were remarkably similar in content. The dynamics of participation in each plan were discussed, and observations and guidance about effective practices that can improve planning processes and result in more effective plans were shared.

Chapter 7 concludes our discussion with a defense of shared governance and a series of suggestions for making it more effective.

CHAPTER

In Defense of Shared Governance

It is not enough to have a good idea.

We began this consideration of governance by recounting the dilemmas of a university president who is expected to be a faculty advocate, be responsive to external needs, and run a tighter ship—pay faculty better, add faculty, support and expand instructional and research programs, make economic development happen, fill workforce needs, keep costs and tuition down, and enhance student learning.

We went on to suggest that external forces have more to say about internal matters than ever before. Market pressures focus attention on profitability and competition. The globalization of science and technology and the growing importance of technology in instruction and research turn intellectual property into a profitable commodity. Institutions compete for students often lacking in preparation, while attempting to respond to increased student mobility and demand for instruction at any time and any place. External demands for accountability change the conversation from what is taught to what is learned. All of these forces and others find states placing different and more complex demands on public higher education while shifting resources to other priorities. These realities challenge all participants in shared governance to understand what it means to be market-smart and to consider whether their priorities are mission-centered; they also require all, but especially institutional leaders, to be politically savvy.

We have taken the view that concentrating attention on any one group of governance participants (faculty, boards, or administrators) does not reflect the realities of governance as an art form. It is the interaction of these participants that characterizes the governance challenges, especially those involved in big issues. Big issues differ from the routine of the academy; they are characterized by conflict, fluid participation, and participant goals that are ambiguous and contested.

We have noted that public boards are inherently political in the way they are appointed. This characteristic can often be reflected in a dislike for deciding controversial matters that pit boards in opposition to students, faculty, or a segment of the community at large. Unions are political/advocacy organizations, especially on behalf of faculty salaries and benefits, although that is not all they are. Faculty senates are representative bodies, but do not necessarily represent all internal constituents; they value deliberation and guard the faculty role in the governance process. And administrators, some more skilled than others, operate in a demanding environment, often not appreciating the importance and complexity of being market-smart, mission-centered, and politically savvy.

Shared decision making among boards, administrators, and faculty is the time-honored standard for deciding institutional issues. However, when issues (even those that fall within the domain of any one party) become highly controversial and morph into wicked problems, politics often trumps the values of the collegium. Parties become staunch advocates and the politics of advocacy takes over. Under advocacy/political systems, perception becomes reality and protection of special interests becomes legitimate behavior.

We argue that for the routine of the academy, and especially for big issues, advocacy systems are not an appropriate alternative decision-making model for higher education. Such systems are modeled after legal principles and characterized by "rules of evidence" rather than a "search for the truth." There is a role for advocacy in any decision-making process. But the values of the academy—the rule of reason, the search for truth, and the canons of professionalism—are at risk when the politics of advocacy prevails. One of the major challenges facing shared governance is that the academy's commitment to fair and open processes can degenerate into granting legitimacy to the politics of advocacy. The advocacy model is not an acceptable alternative to shared governance. What is needed is more unmasking and recognition of just how far special interests should be allowed to take their case. The higher education community would be better served by less defense of interest group issues and more attention to the good of the whole institution.

In our experience, boards, administrators, and faculty are committed to shared governance, but without sufficient appreciation of what it involves and how to bring it about. Sharing is hard! It's easier for something to be all mine or all yours. Sharing requires an understanding of:

- Who should share;
- Why they should share;
- When they should share;
- What should be shared; and
- How fair shares will be determined and disputes resolved.

Shared governance means formulating and implementing meaningful ways to engage large numbers of people in the sharing process. As the cases discussed throughout this book illustrate, the parties to shared governance are many, but we have limited our discussions to faculty, administrators, and boards. These are the major governance partners *who* bear the burden for sharing and making shared governance work.

It bears repeating that the context of each institution's specific history and culture gives it a unique opportunity to practice the art of governance and further its specific mission-centeredness. We agree with Birnbaum's view that, in governance, "there are no quick fixes or magic bullets" (1992, 196). More than 25 years ago, the Carnegie Council on Policy Studies in Higher Education (1980) told us that there was not one future for all institutions, but that higher education had 3,000 futures. So it is when practicing the art of governance.

The remainder of this chapter will consider the *why, when, what,* and *how* of shared governance and will end with observations on behaviors that tend to enhance this governance process. We begin with *why* there should be shared governance. The answer lies in the character of the academy.

THE CHARACTER OF ACADEMIC ORGANIZATIONS

An academic institution has all the characteristics of a large organization, but few of its advantages. In its business and administrative functions, a college/university operates like a bureaucracy. There are rules to be followed, policies to be developed, and a hierarchy to be observed.

In some of the professional functions of colleges/universities, the values of professional control approach the ideal type represented by the term *collegium.* Academic departments tend to be the chief decision unit for promotions, teaching assignments, the shape of the curriculum in the major, whether students are treated as active learners or vessels into which knowledge is poured, and the like. Academic departments are key units in protecting the professional control structure that characterizes academic organizations and makes them unique organizational types.

In some respects, campus faculty senates and separate college/school senates further this manifestation of professional control. Most observers believe that the set of values represented by this professional control is a legitimate basis on which governance can rest. For the most part, criticisms of the academy do not recommend that professional control be eliminated, but rather that it be modified. Rhoades (2005) calls for an academy that is democratically engaged with and accountable to more diverse constituents. Newman, Couturier, and Scurry (2004) refer to an academy more sensitive to the changing nature of the external environment. Kirp (2003) worries that the forces of the market bring inappropriate pressure on the academy and, in some cases, this pressure results in bad educational decisions. And Gumport (2000 and 2001) calls for collaboration in support of the common good and the importance of protecting an institution's educational and social justice values.

We believe, as did Winston Churchill when commenting on democracy, that shared authority in the academy may be the worst form of governance known, except when compared to any of the alternatives. The debate about shared authority in the twenty-first century should be based on a set of assumptions about the academy and the proper bases for legitimate participation in its governance. We agree that society's changing demands will affect the programmatic configuration of many institutions, and this is proper.

But, in its essence, an academic entity *requires* the professional control of its core functions of teaching and research. We concur with Massy (2003) that the fundamental issue facing institutions in the twenty-first century is the enhancement and protection (if the latter is necessary) of its educational and research missions. Effective pursuit of these core missions by decision makers who share authority requires a better understanding of the political culture of specific institutions and the "big" issues before them. The art of governance is political in nature, and no amount of uneasiness among academics can change this fact.

Over the last 30 years, we have become uneasy about some of the language and rhetoric used to attack political terminology in governing the academy. In our teaching, research, and administrative activities, we have seen legitimate demands for more leadership, greater accountability and decisiveness, and greater flexibility portrayed as panaceas for curing the reported governance problems of the academy. We think these demands are fine as far as they go, but stop short of acknowledging the special nature of politics in the academy.

According to Bolman and Deal (1997, 174), "The question is not whether organizations will have politics but rather what kind of politics they will have." They point out that politics can be energizing or debilitating, hostile or constructive, devastating or creative. In short, making politics productive is possible, but not easy. As we have demonstrated in earlier chapters, consensus on the big issues is unlikely. What can be done, however, is to develop a sense of openness, common values, and a fair process; consensus may not result, but action can be taken.

We offer Bolman and Deal's (1997, 163) summary of five propositions that comprise the assumptions underlying the political framework: (1) organizations are coalitions of individuals and interest groups; (2) these groups have enduring differences about values, beliefs, information, interests, and perceptions of reality; (3) the most important decisions are about who gets what—the allocation of resources; (4) enduring differences and scarce resources give conflict an important role and make power the most important resource; and (5) goals and objectives emerge from bargaining, negotiation, and jockeying among stakeholders.

The academy needs to legitimize such terminology as *the principled use of power and influence to achieve the mission of the institution. Positioning* is a rich concept in the literature on politics and is a common term used to acknowledge that many of the problems facing an institution cannot be solved in one legislative session or one academic year. We contend that *positioning* the institution for long-term success is a more, not less, legitimate basis for judging faculty, administration, or board effectiveness than is success in securing annual legislative appropriations, more research grants, or increases in enrollment. The resolution of the most serious issues facing higher education requires consistent direction over a period of years.

Indeed, in our discussion of strategic planning in Chapter 6, we noted that the content of most plans does not vary much over time or from institution to institution. These documents typically talk about issues such as improving quality, enhancing or protecting enrollments, furthering student and staff diversity, and diversifying revenue streams. In fewer cases, strategic plans attempt to identify areas where the institution has or can develop a competitive advantage. In still fewer cases do plans set priorities responsive to public agendas and establish how progress toward these priorities will be measured or how to fund the objectives and actions identified in the plan. Yet we know that the politics of prioritization and implementation are the key ingredients in whether plans have any meaning. In Chapter 6 we pointed out that, without a plan, the budget is the plan, and if the plan is not linked to the budget, then the budget is still the plan. And linking the budget with a plan requires a degree of political savviness that is not recognized in the debate about shared authority.

We make no argument that political symbols/language offer an exclusive or simple course to correct the problems of shared governance. Rather, multiple perspectives are helpful in understanding the economic, cultural, and sociological nature of colleges. We believe that understanding the political nature of the academy will result in more, not less, mission-centeredness. Further, such understanding is necessary if the forces of the market are to be molded and shaped in ways that do not threaten substantially the core missions of teaching and research.

For the governance process to be characterized by the principled use of power and not smash-mouth politics, there needs to be serious attention given to the dynamics of building and sustaining high levels of trust and legitimacy among those who share the governing process—boards, administrators, and faculty. Hamilton (2002, 2006a, 2006b) has written extensively on professional conduct as it relates to faculty autonomy and shared governance. He makes the case that shared governance is a natural consequence of academic freedom, peer review, and the university's mission to create knowledge. It is the tradition of faculty self-governance as exercised through "peer review of professional competence and ethical conduct that is the linchpin of academic freedom in the United States" (2006b, 2–4). Further, the necessity of academic freedom is the basis for the unwritten contract whereby society grants professionals engaged in the creation and dissemination of knowledge autonomy to govern themselves and, for their part, professionals agree to personal and collegial duties to society (2006a).

We agree with Kezar that no amount of restructuring or reorganizing can substitute for the importance of building relationships and trust.

> The evidence from the case studies I conducted is that leadership, trust and relationships supersede structures and process in effective decision making. A governance system can operate with imperfect structures and processes but if leadership is missing and relationships and trust damaged, the governance system will likely fail for lack of direction, motivation, meaning, integrity, a

sense of common purpose, ways to integrate multiple perspectives, open communication, people willing to listen and legitimacy. (Kezar 2004, 42–45)

The suggestions we offer in the final sections of this chapter illustrate the kinds of
actions/principles/strategies necessary in learning the *when*, *what*, and *how* of being
politically savvy—the fundamental building blocks of shared governance. If used
wisely, the suggestions made here can lead to modifications in practice that allow
appropriate responses to the market and other external forces while preserving the
professional control so necessary to effective learning and research missions.

Hamilton (2006b) argues convincingly, and we agree, that shared governance
requires stakeholders (boards, administrators, and faculty) to continually build
social capital and trust within and across their members. Each new generation
of stakeholders needs to renew its understanding of the relationships involved
in the social contract—the academic profession's mission and its relationship to
academic freedom, shared governance, professionalism, and the resulting duties
of the stakeholders (17–19). It cannot be assumed that these relationships and
concepts will be passed from generation to generation through "osmosis-like dif-
fusion" (10). We suggest that modeling politically savvy behaviors and actions is
fundamental to the generation-by-generation renewal of higher education's social
contract and especially to the future of effective shared governance. We begin
with timing practices critical to *when* sharing takes place.

TIMING AND EFFECTIVE ACADEMIC DECISION MAKING

The national higher education community is committed to the notion of
strategic planning that establishes priorities and aids the decision-making process. The assumption is that big decisions, such as the reallocation of resources,
require making forced choices among undesirable alternatives. A forced-choice
decision-making environment puts great attention on the legitimacy and trust
of decision-making processes, including the criteria used to arrive at judgments
about appropriate courses of action. If boards, faculty, and administrators trust
each other, the legitimacy of academic governance is likely to be high and the
effectiveness of decisions will be greater.

The legitimacy of academic governance is based on mutual trust and cooperation
among the participants. Strategic plans that set priorities are essential, but the need
for legitimacy in governance puts increased emphasis on *who can be trusted* to make
the final decisions. If the tone of relations is adversarial and a conflict-of-interest
mentality prevails, then the open information so crucial to effective governance and
planning will not be available to all of the parties. For example, when advocates
control the debate, information becomes a political tool to be used according to the
political advantage it brings rather than for the facts it embodies.

We believe there are five elements relating to timing, or the *when* of the
decision-making process, that help establish and maintain high degrees of openness and trust as colleges and universities seek to make difficult decisions.

Consult early and often. Research has shown that the perceptions of faculty and senior administrators are not always as different as some might suspect. This means that progress may occur more smoothly if these key participants discuss their roles and perspectives and attempt to resolve their differences early in the change process (Eckel 2003, 158–159).

Participants in a problem or issue must have a chance to consider the formulation of alternatives, as well as the phrasing of issues, before the preferred alternative becomes rigidified. One of the most common examples of attempts to provide early consultation is the practice of appointing ad hoc committees or study groups to conduct feasibility studies. These groups can be effective means to illuminate problems and consider fruitful approaches to solving them. But care must be taken to phrase the request for advice carefully. Feasibility committees should not be used to confirm decisions already made—to do so threatens the legitimacy of other such efforts. If a decision has been made, it is wiser to appoint a committee to help implement the decision rather than to study its feasibility.

Engage in joint formulation of procedures. An agreement on the appropriate process to be followed is a vital part of relationships built on trust and joint endeavor. It is crucial that the process be perceived as fair. In the Mythical State case discussed in Chapter 5, the committee process laid out by the president was not perceived to be fair given a related responsibility assigned to, albeit not exercised by, an existing committee. General agreement about process may involve such decisions as whether to hold hearings on the issue, whom to consult, and whether the eventual advice is to be confidential or not. There are some issues (for example, personnel matters) where the results must be held in strictest confidence. It should be clear, however, that excessive claims for confidentiality threaten basic relationships of trust.

Allow time to formulate responses. A common source of irritation for participants in college and university governance is the request for advice that has to be rendered immediately. Although many such requests are legitimate because of a deadline imposed from the outside, too often such requests merely reflect sloppy planning or inadequate anticipation of problems. It is a lack of political savviness not to understand that too many requests for quick advice will kill the trust necessary for effective governance. Too many unreasonable deadlines—appointing committees and expecting them to complete their work just before a summer break—are a constant source of irritation in governance.

What, then, are reasonable time constraints for rendering or getting appropriate advice and counsel? We believe that certain of the more controversial resource allocation issues are linked to the budget cycle. And most annual budget decisions are on a fixed schedule well known to some participants, but not well understood by others. Regular communications about that cycle will help make it clear which deadlines are fixed and which are flexible. The schedule will vary depending on institutional cultures and purposes, but generally it is known well in advance. We recognize that some cases require multiple perspectives that include consideration of the year you are in, the one you are preparing for, and the separation of capital and operating budgets. These complexities are manageable, but clear communication requires that they be acknowledged, understood, and regarded as legitimate.

Make information available in a timely manner. Those who want to restrict the free flow of information in academic affairs should be prepared to justify that restriction. The presumption should be openness. The budgets of public institutions are often public documents, for example, and the only remaining question is how much detail must be made available. Few reports or data speak to personalities, and most of these reports can be formulated to concentrate on the issues.

As a practical matter, some argue that freely available information causes more problems than it is worth. People get buried in paper, administrators have to spend too much time generating reports to justify discrepancies, and so forth. People suffer from process fatigue. These arguments are unpersuasive when put beside the need to establish trust and legitimacy. Information can be fully available to those who want it, assuming that such requests are reasonable—that is, they do not take excessive staff time. Not everyone will want to see everything, so it is possible to be selective on some matters and provide information upon request.

Provide adequate feedback. The basic principle of shared governance should be that, when a decision is made, it is communicated to the people who rendered advice and counsel and to the community at large. In cases where disagreements occur, these should be discussed with the recommending body so that they are fully understood and the reasons for the disagreements are clear. Adequate feedback is crucial if the organizations and the people in them are to learn how to do things better. Administrators need to say why advice was or was not taken, and faculty members need to share some of the complexities inherent in a world of forced choices. Some of the difficulties encountered in the student transfer case might have been minimized had the administration utilized meetings in addition to memoranda to communicate why some of the advice given could not be taken. In Chapter 6 we discussed how the existence of electronic mail made it possible for participants to learn why some proposed changes to strategic plan drafts were used and others were not. The communication of rationale, not the lack thereof, accounted in large part for the difference in perception that one plan was bottom up and another was not.

We are concerned with the arguments that the process of establishing priorities or making cuts in academic programs is somehow beyond the ability of faculty committees. Eckel's (2000) study of the "hard decision" to discontinue academic programs at four institutions suggests otherwise. We are optimistic that faculty committees operating in open atmospheres of trust and legitimacy will be effective participants in the difficult judgments about academic vitality and even cuts. Some argue that the use of faculty committees in this context is excessively cumbersome and will degenerate into a fight to protect one's home department. Indeed, in some cases faculty unions and senates have refused or discouraged participation in budget cutting or retrenchment exercises because they believe it divides their membership.

It is generally agreed that finalizing priorities among a variety of choices is an administrative-board responsibility, but faculty advice and counsel are crucial if the process is to be done well and if the choices made are to be intelligent and well informed. We believe that faculty advice is useful and appropriate even when deciding "whose ox is to be gored." In such cases, it may be quite appropriate for the committees to concentrate on the procedures, methods, and criteria to be used to arrive at priority decisions. For example, what criteria should be used in assessing the quality of academic programs? What process should be followed in creating or closing programs? Eckel's (2000, 33) research "refutes the belief that more authority for administrators will lead to better institutional decision making."

In short, the timing associated with the decision-making process is critical. A well-ordered, open process that is perceived as fair to all the various parties will enhance the legitimacy and trust so necessary for effective *shared* campus governance. We now turn our attention to the *what* of shared governance.

WHAT IS TO BE SHARED

It must be clear that systems of shared governance do not mean that boards and administrators are freed from the responsibility to make decisions. There are, however, at least six elements to be shared.

The opportunity to participate. Some faculty members and students are eager to seize this opportunity simply because they are interested and share a commitment to making the institution function more effectively. Some view participation as part of their professional responsibility. Others see it as an opportunity to further their own interests or the interests of their departments.

Access to information necessary for effective participation. We have discussed the importance of making critical information available in a timely manner. Here we stress that all parties have a responsibility to make available pertinent and accurate information. Administrators, in particular, bear a heavy burden to make complex information available in concise and readily understood formats.

Access to decision makers. Access is one of the more important and least understood factors in governance. The opportunity to consult or talk with the dean, the president, other administrators, or the governing board can be an important source of informal influence. In our experience, involved but busy faculty and student leaders rarely miss attending scheduled sessions or informal gatherings with presidents and boards. Fitting in "access time" on busy executive calendars is more of a necessity than a luxury.

The opportunity to be influential. This is, of course, difficult to estimate, but it is a factor in the motivation of many individuals to participate in campus governance. The fact that individuals have been asked to advise key leaders in the institution is in itself an important status symbol on many campuses.

The responsibility to adopt a perspective broader than one's own (narrowly defined) interests. In some institutions this is itself controversial. We pointed out in Chapter 3, for example, that individual trustees have the obligation to see the interests of the college as a whole rather than to pursue special interests in board deliberations. We would make the same argument for faculty participating in college or campus-wide committees. We noted in Chapter 4 that one of the most common examples of the necessity to see broader university interests occurs in debates over general education. Many times those debates involve a department's campaign to get its courses included as part of the general education requirement. Because no department is solely responsible for the general need to develop critical thinking skills, these attributes of an educated person are not well articulated in the undergraduate curriculum. College and departmental advocates can become so focused on the needs of their unit, a perceived mandate, or outcomes that the data appear to support, that they can lose sight of the good of the whole, be insensitive to plausible alternatives, or disregard legitimate concerns about quality.

The responsibility to take at least some of the advice received. It is important to understand that those who continually reject the advice received risk attacks on the legitimacy of the process. In cases where the recommendations are complex, it would be useful to stress those parts of the reasoning behind the recommendation that are acceptable rather than those parts that are unacceptable. This observation applies as well to relationships between presidents and provosts, as we argued in Chapter 5.

OBSERVATIONS ABOUT THE *HOW* OF SHARED GOVERNANCE

It is relatively easy for us to describe the characteristics of an effective process and the nature of shared responsibility. These are documented in the literature, and we have contributed to this discussion in other contexts (Mortimer and McConnell 1978). In practice, however, academic governance is an art, not a science. As it actually functions, it is an ambiguous process full of loose ends and personal judgments. In this section we discuss this ambiguity.

That faculty and administrators often see themselves at sea amid forces beyond their control is a major threat to the effectiveness of an academic management system. We are persuaded that those institutions that retain their mission-centeredness and increase their vitality will be those that are proactive in dealing with environmental turbulence and the influence of external events. The fact is that many of the challenges facing institutions can be dealt with effectively. To this end we offer some advice.

Facing problems is usually better than hoping they will blow over. Put another way, the cost of failing to solve problems has jumped dramatically. For example, institutions that find themselves in regions where there is a substantial drop or increase in the college-age population have to develop responses to their demographics. What will it mean to the institution if more part-time students enroll and a majority of their eventual graduates are transfer students? Is the institution willing to adjust schedules to accommodate students who can only enroll late in the day? Will the institution work with feeder institutions to make the transfer process predictable for students and avoid unnecessarily extending the time it takes to graduate? Will the institution deal with the intellectual property issues inherent in using technology for instructional delivery?

Do it right the first time. Cleaning up after internal or external blunders takes a great deal more time than doing it right the first time. The importance of process is that it clarifies alternatives and allows more careful consideration of questions such as who needs to be consulted about the decision, what are the strengths and weaknesses of certain alternatives, and what are the implementation problems. An orderly process will help avoid at least some blunders.

Facing problems does not always mean solving them. All problems do not have solutions. In many cases, the solutions are more costly than the problem. For example, the school closure case could have been resolved by an infusion of about $1 million and the faculty would have been happy; however, the administration believed that $1 million would not solve the accreditation agency's concerns about lack of research productivity.

Do it yourself. It is generally better for all concerned to handle the matter themselves rather than to have something forced on them by external parties. The golden rule is: "Do unto yourself what you would not have others do unto you lest they really mess things up." This is particularly appropriate for boards, administrators, and faculty working in state systems of higher education or in multicampus systems. A good rule is to keep decisions on campus rather than to refer them to parties beyond the control of the campus. Principles of academic freedom and individual choice are better protected by the parties involved in them than would be the case if issues are referred to higher levels or external bodies for resolution. For example, a campus leader within a system who forwards for board approval an updated campus general education core when there is no policy requiring board action establishes a precedent. All future general education modifications by any campus will now very likely require board action.

Deciding how to do something should be a crucial ingredient in deciding whether to do it. The process of implementing a decision may be as important as the process of arriving at it and the actual decision itself. To think about the strategy of implementation is not to be without concern for the substance of the decision. To be effective, one must be thoughtful about substance, but one must also be concerned about the attitudes and interests of various subordinates and colleagues. Some institutions neglect to consult middle managers about whether changes can be implemented at reasonable costs and within reasonable time lines. Failure to get assessments about such important matters can cripple the intent of the decision. Scholars talk about the unintended consequences of decisions. Once a decision is made, the energy of the decision makers tends to dissipate, and its implementation is put in the hands of people who may be uninformed about the actual purpose of the decision.

People agree more readily about problems than solutions. If you can gain agreement about the nature of critical problems and the importance of addressing them, solutions are more likely to follow. For example, a tenure quota is often a solution offered by those who are really concerned about declining flexibility in financial resources or the need to respond more rapidly to changes in student demand. If the problem really is fiscal flexibility, or an inflexible faculty profile, tenure quotas may not be an appropriate solution. Certainly discussions about how to increase flexibility should examine alternatives (in addition to a tenure quota) that might turn out to be more effective.

Timing is essential. The importance of process is that it gives people some time for mental digestion when dealing with change. Put another way, the advantage of a number of ideas may be immediately obvious while the disadvantages take time to ferret out. Part of the essence of effective change is giving people time to digest it fully.

Stop shooting from the hip. Scholars who would be appalled at "gut" statements in their disciplines often have no hesitation when making thoughtless comments about teaching, students, the administration, the outside world, and other matters involved in university governance. We need data, examples, analyses, test cases, and pilot projects. One of the chief tasks of those who administer is to challenge the entire university to bring an objective and constructive style to bear on its own problems. We cannot substitute quantitative judgments where qualitative ones are required, but we can develop a tradition of scholarly and thoughtful analysis. We need to remember that, even in administrative matters, we are always teaching. Students who see us act in ways that are not scholarly learn from us. In this sense everyone in the institution is an educator.

No single leadership style ensures success. Consistency is needed so people will know what to expect, but it is possible to continue to learn and grow by adopting useful elements from many styles and by using the methods appropriate to particular circumstances. For example, some committees expect that the chair will take responsibility for directing activities, proposing alternatives, and managing the affairs of the committee. In short, they look to the chair for decisive leadership in resolving committee dilemmas. In other contexts, the committee chair is expected to manage consensus rather than provide direction. In such cases, it may be that an organized discussion is a more effective way to proceed rather than to simply propose a course of action. The key to effective governance is to be able to understand and operate in both contexts.

There is a difference between being committed and investing a proposal with one's ego. It is usually a mistake to make any plan a matter of personal success or failure—to do so makes the planner vulnerable and may destroy any chance for objectivity. The essence of effective leadership is to turn proposals into "the other person's idea." The true measure of success is when one hears others—faculty, administrators, board members, or community leaders—advance your ideas and suggestions as their own.

Progress may not be a straight line. Be prepared to take two steps forward and one step back or sideways. Progress is probably more usefully conceptualized as "running against the wind" in a sailboat race.

Good logic is often an insufficient argument. It is a difficult lesson for all parties in shared governance to learn that *it is not enough to have a good idea.* Many people come to a discussion about a policy or program with such deeply held feelings that they are unwilling to consider alternatives. Then we must think about ways to create an atmosphere of inquiry and interest. One cannot assume (as was the mistake in the student transfer case) that what seems on the surface to be an obviously good idea will be understood by others in the same light.

OBSERVATIONS ABOUT OPEN SYSTEMS
Open Systems and Leadership

To build essential patterns of legitimacy and trust, the approach to governance should be characterized by a high degree of openness—open plans, open policy statements, open reasons, open procedures, and fair informal and formal processes. The reason for repeating the word *open* is a powerful one—it is a natural opponent of arbitrariness and a natural ally in the struggle to build trust and legitimacy in academic governance. An open system of governance is more likely to be both fair and effective. The danger of an open system, however, is that no one will make the decisions, so it is important to think about how such a system should work.

Listening is not the same as losing control. Most of us fear that encouraging participation will lead to losing control of the problem. It is important to remember that people want to be heard, not to have their lives or programs arbitrarily altered from afar. The desire to be heard is not the same as wanting the responsibility for making the decision or achieving results. Some will be relieved that controversial decisions are not theirs to make. There will always be those who, despite the opportunity to be heard, will second guess. To encourage participation and to be open to alternatives does not mean that one gives up the responsibility to make decisions or is required to do what people say. Openness means listening and considering advice seriously; it does not mean asking for a decision from a constituency or interest group.

Perfect communication rarely happens. An open system depends on the availability of information; however, not everyone listens. Many will not take the time to become informed, and one cannot and should not expect perfect communication. What is required is continuing and effective communication, including information about constraints in the process or in the substance of the decision.

Openness is required, but so is leadership, and outstanding leadership creates consensus and does not merely "hope to find it." Consensus without leadership has no direction. The consensus that is crucial is that the process has been fair. Many people do not want to be leaders or make decisions. Many slip into the role of permanent critic, naysayer, or cynic and prefer that role. An open system makes this painfully apparent, and all partners in shared governance have a responsibility to understand it.

An important task of leadership at all levels is setting the agenda and tone of discussions. A good agenda reflects initiative, and there is a difference between initiative and authority. Initiative is more important, but everyone argues over authority. Most of administration is reactive; little is initiative, but it is with initiative that real gains are made. In setting an agenda one can generate an understanding that something can be done, as well as set a tone of civility. If one can gain agreement about the nature of critical problems and the importance of addressing them, solutions will flow. It is important to help people arrive at a tolerance of the likelihood that not all solutions will be exactly what they would propose. It is important, however, that the agenda points toward shared goals.

Colleges and universities need more and better leadership at all levels—not just from presidents and vice presidents, but from deans, department chairs, faculty, student affairs officers, student leadership, everyone—and in all endeavors—teaching, research, and administration. There is not a fixed amount of power to be divided up among contending parties. An organization of strong leaders has more power and accomplishes more. Good leadership engenders good followers. All parties in shared governance must be leaders and followers simultaneously. Good followers have the capacity to differ or oppose in a constructive manner.

The degree of consultation depends on the time frame of the problem, and time frames can be communicated. An emergency with a short time frame requires a different approach, but even in such circumstances the constraints of the case can be communicated. Ideally, consultation must begin early in the process, not after decisions have been reached or after a problem has been created. But the form of consultation will vary depending on the nature of the problem and the traditions of the institution. Whatever the form and timing of consultation, communicating the results is important.

If you develop recognition of the need for change and the expectation that change will come and then fail to perform, you will create a credibility problem. For example, once the expectation is created that an open and consultative process will be used, a failure to consult will cause disillusionment. The illusion of openness without the reality (e.g., consulting about a decision already made or providing too short a time for consultation) is irritating. An open system appears to be slow and requires patience. But if blunders are averted, it will in fact help one reach the desired goal more quickly.

The Challenges of Open Systems

We acknowledge that there are several potential problems with operating in a system where information is openly shared. These issues are manageable but constitute important challenges.

Special interests may use advance notice to mobilize opposition. Because they often have greater resources than individual participants, special interest groups (segments of the administration, unions, groups of deans or department chairs, public interest groups, or agencies of state government) may mobilize on certain sides of an issue. Those familiar with the debate about student access policy at public universities realize that any suggestion of tuition increases results in organized interest group activity on the part of some students and public groups.

Few individuals enter the ranks of university faculty with an interest in campus governance. Active faculty colleagues can easily dominate issues and sometimes discourage participation by others. It is useful to conceive of the faculty as a political system composed roughly of disinterested actors (50% to 60%), spectators (30% to 40%), and activists (5% to 10%). This typology of faculty participation in governance simply acknowledges that many are not interested in this aspect of the institution or their professional lives. Most of the spectators believe it is necessary to participate to fulfill their professional responsibility. It is important to know who the activists are and how they operate. Some are committed faculty members with a sincere concern for the preservation and interpretation of faculty and academic values. They accept faculty participation in governance as a professional responsibility, perform it well, and continue to be chosen to positions of prominence by their colleagues.

Unfortunately, in some cases a minority of individuals with ideological commitments get into positions of influence or insert themselves from the sidelines. Often they are able to take advantage of the general tolerance of the academic community, which encourages every viewpoint to be heard, to succeed in tying up the process. If ideologues are not dealt with effectively, the academy's tolerance for divergent points of view can be a crippling problem.

Administrators, boards, and faculty leaders should be encouraged to "discipline" or deal with obstructionists. Often a word from a colleague can be more effective than any communication or discussion with an administrator. Some institutions have found it effective to make sure that such individuals have plenty to do. For example, critics must be challenged to do more than criticize—they must be challenged to propose solutions that are workable in the context of the institution involved.

As seasoned observers of the academic scene have cynically observed, "Put unreasonable people together and let them hash out the problems." There is a touch of wisdom in this comment; it recognizes that in some cases demands may be unreasonable or solutions unworkable. In such cases, one effective way to deal with the situation is to have those who oppose each other work out proposals for the rest of the people to consider.

Differences accumulate. Another major danger in openness is that value differences can be cumulative and result in divisive, permanent rifts in the academic community. There is an old saying that "friends come and go, but enemies accumulate." Sharp disagreements between people with widely divergent views tend to accumulate and persist over time. The danger is that these disputes become so ingrained in the academic and administrative culture of the institution that discussants fail to listen to each other. A common generalization is, "If that person is for a proposal, I am against it, before I even hear it." It must be acknowledged that any large social system has some basic differences. Clark Kerr has been said to observe that "10 percent of the people are unhappy all of the time about everything."

In fact, such important issues as whether merit pay can be administered fairly, or the relative balance between general and professional education in curricular affairs, are legitimate academic debates. They are only disruptive to the extent that the disputes tend to line the advocates up consistently on a variety of issues so that the parties become entrenched. Board members, administrators, and faculty must adopt the attitude, in combating such entrenchment, that there are no victories, only carefully derived solutions. It is important to look for win-win solutions because the notion of winners and losers creates difficult problems for the losers. Losers must somehow get even or accept their losing status. Winners tend to forget that all can be lost in the implementation process. If losers work hard during the implementation stage to gain back some of their losses, the full intent of a solution or proposed change is likely to be unrealized. Neither alternative is productive in communities built on high levels of trust and legitimacy.

A win-win solution is depicted in a situation where a proposal or solution emerges from the group as the genuine consensus after all of the views have been heard. In such situations, even those departments or colleges whose status or position may have been diminished recognize that the larger interests of the whole have been well served.

Professional judgments are subjective. Open systems of governance run the danger of being a victim of the tyranny of objective or measurable variables or results. In our zeal to be open and objective, we may forget that, in their essence, professional judgments are subjective. They rely on peer judgments about whose teaching is really effective, what education is "good," or what should be the appropriate balance of course offerings.

Our view is that the conduct of professional affairs is so complex that it is impossible to fashion rules to cover every circumstance. For example, comprehensive faculty evaluation systems can clarify criteria for promotion and tenure and specify their priority. But they cannot eliminate the necessity for professional judgment—nor should they.

Yet it is almost a truism that, without measures of educational effectiveness, efficiency measures will carry the day. The "objective" criteria of time in rank, seniority, and student/faculty ratios tend to dominate the decision-making milieu, simply because they may be easier to quantify. A similar situation exists when considering the addition of new programs. Although there are many objective measures to consider, in the end the decision to add programs or levels of instruction is a judgment call. It is the essence of an effective academic governance process to work hard on criteria and procedures that allow and encourage the exercise of genuine academic judgment.

Open priorities are needed, but they will cause grief. A particularly difficult challenge within open systems is setting open priorities. The problem is that some people or programs come to realize that they are not high priorities. We are not sure that any programs or people should be told they are low priorities, but it is our experience that the failure to be recognized as a high priority can result in low morale.

In times of decline it is good to have a supportive spouse because one has few friends when budgets are cut. Those who are losing funds and resources will seldom think it is fair. For example, deans are committed to healthy schools and colleges. They believe it is a lack of wisdom that causes campus-wide administrators to put pressure on units merely because enrollments are waning. Under systems of strategic choice, it is difficult to persuade low priority areas of the wisdom of outcomes that result in their lower priority standing. And it is fairly rare for higher priority areas to publicly agree that their colleagues in other units should be a low priority.

On the other hand, because a major share of the reallocated money goes to pay the hidden costs of energy and fringe benefits, those associated with programs that are identified as high priorities want to know where all the money went! And if the situation is so bad that priority areas have to take *lesser* cuts, don't expect them to appreciate this largesse. It is also the case that funds usually cannot be reallocated fast enough to handle shifts in enrollment that occur when students change their preference patterns. Built-in rigidities in the faculty personnel system, for example, may work against rapid deployment of faculty resources into areas that experience marked gains in enrollment or priority over a short period of time.

Finally, we would acknowledge that there are some matters in academic affairs that should be confidential. The precise definition of such matters will often be a matter of local culture—for example, whether or not salaries are public information. Some situations, such as union negotiations, often call for confidentiality while negotiations are in process. Even in such situations, both sides would gain and the institution would benefit if the natural gamesmanship involved in collective bargaining with faculty and staff were removed or at least minimized.

Overall, effective shared governance requires open systems in which boards, administrators, and faculty understand the political skills needed to make it work. These same shared governance partners must also understand and counter the efforts and behaviors that cause open decision-making environments to be unwieldy and unworkable.

CONCLUDING COMMENTS

This book is about the art of governance and argues that the *how* of decisions may well be as important as the *what*. The cumulative effect of markets, technology, globalization, mobile students, and accountability make the practice of shared governance crucial if market-smart, mission-centered, and politically savvy higher educational institutions are to flourish. The principles and advice in this chapter argue for the principled use of power directed toward the end of enhancing the educational, research, and service missions of institutions. We repeat the proposition that, in many respects, colleges and universities are political entities. The only question is what kind of politics is practiced.

To the reader, this book undoubtedly seems to describe more potential problems in academic governance that it does potential solutions. Our experience suggests that this imbalance is an accurate reflection of reality. Politically savvy practitioners of governance recognize this imbalance and try to compensate for it. They do this by constantly striving to anticipate potential problems and working to avoid or solve them before they become big, messy issues. We believe that this sort of anticipatory problem management may represent the highest form of politically savvy behavior.

There is no simple checklist of how to be politically savvy; we believe it is an art form, not a science. The fair and open processes we have described, together with some of the tactics cited, need to be internalized by those who participate in the art of governance. Adept decision makers rarely just appear; excellent mentoring and role models are critical. Politically savvy skills and knowledge are more readily internalized and available when needed if one has had the good fortune to observe them practiced by competent and experienced leaders. Providing those new to governance—be they board members, faculty leaders, or administrators—the opportunity to observe how strategies and tactics can emerge and help solve wicked problems is an overlooked but essential component of good governance.

We end by returning to the importance of understanding the role that politically savvy behavior plays in implementation. A decision in itself changes nothing. When a decision is made, we rarely know if it is good or bad. We must wait for it to be implemented and its consequences to become clear. We spend more time living with the consequences of our decisions than we do in making those decisions. As a result, those interested in the art of governance—in getting things done—need to spend more time learning to master the craft of making things work. Good ideas abound—making good ideas work is another matter altogether and requires a great deal of politically savvy behavior. To do the good, meritorious work of educating students, it is essential that the faculty, administrators, and boards share the governance of the academy. They need to take responsibility as a whole for the governance of their institution as a whole.

REFERENCES

American Association of University Professors. N.d.a. *Evaluation of shared governance*. Retrieved March 5, 2006, from http://www.aaup.org/governance/resources/govevaluation.htm.

———. N.d.b. *Traits of effective senates*. Retrieved January 30, 2006, from http://www.aaup.org/governance/resources/ttrraits.htm.

———. 2001. *Policy Documents and Reports*. 9th ed. Washington, D.C.: American Association of University Professors.

American Federation of Teachers. 2002. *Shared Governance in Colleges and Universities*. Washington, D.C.: American Federation of Teachers.

American Federation of Teachers and National Education Association. 2004. *The Truth about Unions and Shared Governance*. Washington, D.C.: American Federation of Teachers and National Education Association.

Annunziato, F. R. 1994. Faculty strikes in higher education: 1966–1994 [Electronic version]. *National Center for the Study of Collective Bargaining in Higher Education and the Professions Newsletter* 22 (4).

Association of American Colleges and Universities. 2006. *Academic freedom and educational responsibility*. AAC&U board of directors' statement. Retrieved August 23, 2006, from http://www.aacu.org/about/statements/academic_freedom.cfm.

Association of Governing Boards of Universities and Colleges. 1984. *Presidents Make a Difference: Strengthening Leadership in Colleges and Universities. A Report of the Commission on Strengthening Presidential Leadership*. Washington, D.C.: Association of Governing Boards of Universities and Colleges.

———. 1996. *Renewing the Academic Presidency: Stronger Leadership for Tougher Times*. Report of the Commission on the Academic Presidency. Washington, D.C.: Association of Governing Boards of Universities and Colleges.

———. 1998. *Bridging the Gap between State Government and Public Higher Education*. Washington, D.C.: Association of Governing Boards of Universities and Colleges.

―――. 1999. *AGB Statement on Institutional Governance*. Washington, D.C.: Association of Governing Boards of Universities and Colleges.

―――. 2001. *Governing in the Public Trust: External Influences on Colleges and Universities*. Washington, D.C.: Association of Governing Boards of Universities and Colleges.

―――. 2003. *Merit Screening of Citizens for Gubernatorial Appointment to Public College and University Trusteeship*. State Policy Brief no. 1. Washington, D.C.: Association of Governing Boards of Universities and Colleges.

Baldridge, J. V., D. V. Curtis, G. P. Ecker, and G. L. Riley. 1977. "Alternative Models of Governance in Higher Education." In *Governing Academic Organizations*, eds. G. L. Riley and J. V. Baldridge, 2–25. Berkeley, Calif.: McCutchan.

Barefoot, B. 2003. "Taking Longer to Graduate." *Trusteeship* (May/June): 34–35.

Bastedo, M. N. 2005. "The Making of an Activist Governing Board." *The Review of Higher Education* 28 (4): 551–70.

Benjamin, R., and S. Carroll. 1998. "The Implications of the Changed Environment for Governance in Higher Education." In *The Responsive University: Restructuring for High Performance*, ed. W. G. Tierney, 92–119. Baltimore, Md.: The Johns Hopkins University Press.

Berra, Y. 1998. *The Yogi Book: I Really Didn't Say Everything I Said!* New York: Workman Publishing Company.

Birnbaum, R. 1988. *How Colleges Work: The Cybernetics of Academic Organization and Leadership*. San Francisco: Jossey-Bass.

―――. 1989. "The Latent Organizational Functions of the Academic Senate." *Journal of Higher Education* 60 (4): 232–43.

―――. 1992. *How Academic Leadership Works: Understanding Success and Failure in the College Presidency*. San Francisco: Jossey-Bass.

―――. 2000. *Management Fads in Higher Education: Where They Come from, What They Do, Why They Fail*. San Francisco: Jossey-Bass.

―――. 2004. "The End of Shared Governance: Looking Ahead or Looking Back." In *Restructuring Shared Governance in Higher Education*, eds. W. G. Tierney and V. M. Lechuga, 5–22. New Directions for Higher Education no. 127. San Francisco: Jossey-Bass.

Blumenstyk, G. 1998. Berkeley pact with a Swiss company takes technology transfer to a new level [Electronic version]. *The Chronicle of Higher Education* (December 11).

―――. 2001. A vilified corporate partnership produces little change (except better facilities) [Electronic version]. *The Chronicle of Higher Education* (June 22).

Blustain, H., P. Goldstein, and G. Lozier. 1999. "Assessing the New Competitive Landscape." In *Dancing with the Devil: Information Technology and the New Competition in Higher Education*, eds. R. N. Katz and Associates, 51–71. San Francisco: Jossey-Bass.

Bolman, L. G., and T. E. Deal. 1997. *Reframing Organizations: Artistry, Choice, and Leadership*. 2nd ed. San Francisco: Jossey-Bass.

Bornstein, R. 2003. *Legitimacy in the Academic Presidency*. Westport, Conn.: Praeger.

Breneman, D. W. 2004. *Are the States and Public Higher Education Striking a New Bargain?* Public Policy Paper Series no. 04–02. Washington, D.C.: Association of Governing Boards of Universities and Colleges.

Carey, K. 2004. *A Matter of Degrees: Improving Graduation Rates in Four-Year Colleges and Universities*. Washington, D.C.: The Education Trust.

Carnegie Council on Policy Studies in Higher Education. 1980. *Three Thousand Futures: The Next Twenty Years for Higher Education*. San Francisco: Jossey-Bass.

Center for Higher Education Policy Analysis. 2003. *Challenges for Governance: A National Report*. Los Angeles: University of Southern California.

Chaffee, E. E. 1985. "Three Models of Strategy." *Academy of Management Review* 10 (1): 89–98.

Chait, R. P., T. P. Holland, and B. E. Taylor. 1991. *The Effective Board of Trustees*. New York: American Council on Education and Macmillan.

———. 1996. *Improving the Performance of Governing Boards*. Westport, Conn.: American Council on Education and Oryx Press.

Cohen, M. D., and J. G. March. 1974. *Leadership and Ambiguity: The American College President*. A general report prepared for The Carnegie Commission on Higher Education. New York: McGraw-Hill.

Cope, R. G. 1981. *Strategic Planning, Management, and Decision Making*. AAHE-ERIC/ Higher Education Research Report no. 9. Washington, D.C.: American Association for Higher Education.

Corrigan, M. E. 2002. *The American College President: 2002 edition*. Washington, D.C.: American Council on Education.

Couturier, L. K. 2006. *Checks and balances at work: The restructuring of Virginia's public higher education system*. Retrieved July 31, 2006, from http://www.highereducation. org/reports/checks_balances/exec_summary.shtml.

Crowley, J. N. 1994. *No Equal in the World: An Interpretation of the Academic Presidency*. Reno, Nev.: University of Nevada Press.

Currie, J., R. DeAngelis, H. de Boer, J. Huisman, and C. Lacotte. 2003. *Globalizing Practices and University Responses: European and Anglo-American Differences*. Westport, Conn.: Praeger.

Dickeson, R. C. 1999. *Prioritizing Academic Programs and Services: Reallocating Resources to Achieve Strategic Balance*. San Francisco: Jossey-Bass.

Duderstadt, J. J. 1999. "Can Colleges and Universities Survive in the Information Age?" In *Dancing with the Devil: Information Technology and the New Competition in Higher Education*, eds. R. N. Katz and Associates, 1–25. San Francisco: Jossey-Bass.

Duderstadt, J. J., and F. W. Womack. 2003. *The Future of the Public University in America: Beyond the Crossroads*. Baltimore, Md.: The Johns Hopkins University Press.

Duryea, E. D. 2000. *The Academic Corporation: A History of College and University Governing Boards*. Ed. D. Williams. New York: Falmer Press.

Eckel, P. D. 2000. "The Role of Shared Governance in Institutional Hard Decisions: Enabler or Antagonist?" *The Review of Higher Education* 24 (1): 15–39.

———. 2003. "Are They Singing from the Same Hymn Book?" In *Connecting the Dots … the Essence of Planning: The Best of Planning for Higher Education 1997–2003*, ed. Rod Rose, 153–59. Ann Arbor, Mich.: Society for College and University Planning.

Eckel, P. D., and A. Kezar. 2003. *Taking the Reins: Institutional Transformation in Higher Education*. Westport, Conn.: Praeger.

Education Commission of the States. 1997. *1997 State Postsecondary Education Structures Sourcebook: State Coordinating and Governing Boards*. Denver: Education Commission of the States.

Ehrenberg, R. G., ed. 2004. *Governing Academia*. Ithaca, N.Y.: Cornell University Press.

Ehrenberg, R. G., D. B. Klaff, A. T. Kezsbom, and M. P. Nagowski. 2004. "Collective Bargaining in American Higher Education." In *Governing Academia*, ed. R. G. Ehrenberg, 209–32. Ithaca, N.Y.: Cornell University Press.

Evans, K. 2004. *Common Sense Rules of Advocacy for Lawyers*. St. Paul, Minn.: West Publishing Co.

Ewell, P. 2006. *Making the Grade: How Boards Can Ensure Academic Quality*. Washington, D.C.: Association of Governing Boards of Universities and Colleges.

Fain, P. 2006a. "Renegades Shake Up Trustee Elections." *The Chronicle of Higher Education* (March 10): A25-A26.

———. 2006b. U. of Colorado regents delegate power to administrators in hopes of focusing on major policy issues [Electronic version]. *The Chronicle of Higher Education* (June 8).

Field, K. 2006. Navy lab at U. of Hawai'i gets broadside from critics: Foes say academic integrity would be compromised by military's goals [Electronic version]. *The Chronicle of Higher Education* (February 10).

Fisher, J. L. 1991. *The Board and the President*. New York: American Council on Education and Macmillan.

Freedman, J. O. 2004. "Presidents and Trustees." In *Governing Academia*, ed. R. G. Ehrenberg, 9–27. Ithaca, N.Y.: Cornell University Press.

Fretwell, E. K., Jr. 2000. *System Heads, Boards, and State Officials: More than Management*. Occasional Paper no. 45. Washington, D.C.: Association of Governing Boards of Universities and Colleges.

Gaff, J. G., with B. Puzon. 2000. What if the faculty *really do* assume responsibility for the instructional program. Unpublished manuscript.

Gayle, D. J., B. Tewarie, and A. Q. White, Jr. 2003. *Governance in the Twenty-First-Century University: Approaches to Effective Leadership and Strategic Management*. ASHE-ERIC Higher Education Report 30 (1). San Francisco: Jossey-Bass.

Gerber, L. G. 1997. "Reaffirming the Value of Shared Governance." *Academe* 83 (5): 14–18.

———. 2001. "Inextricably linked": Shared governance and academic freedom [Electronic version]. *Academe* 87 (3).

Gregorian, V. 2005. "Six Challenges to the American University." In *Declining by Degrees: Higher Education at Risk*, eds. R. H. Hersh and J. Merrow, 77–96. New York: Palgrave Macmillan.

Gumport, P. J. 2000. *Academic Governance: New Light on Old Issues*. Occasional Paper no. 42. Washington D.C.: Association of Governing Boards of Universities and Colleges.

———. 2001. "Restructuring: Imperatives and Opportunities for Academic Leaders." *Innovative Higher Education* 25 (4): 239–51.

Gumport, P. J., and B. Pusser. 1997. *Restructuring the Academic Environment*. Stanford, Calif.: Stanford University National Center for Postsecondary Improvement.

Hamilton, N. W. 2002. *Academic Ethics: Problems and Materials on Professional Conduct and Shared Governance*. Westport, Conn.: Praeger Publishers.

———. 2006a. Faculty professionalism: Failures of socialization and the road to loss of professional autonomy [Electronic version]. *Liberal Education* (Fall).

———. 2006b. The future of shared governance. Unpublished manuscript.

Harvey, B. C. 2003. "The Perils of Planning before You Are Ready." In *Connecting the Dots ... the Essence of Planning: The Best of Planning for Higher Education 1997–2003*, ed. Rod Rose, 233–40. Ann Arbor, Mich.: Society for College and University Planning.

Hayes, A. B. 1997. "Shaping the Leadership Team: The President, Governing Board, and Chief Academic Officer." In *First among Equals: The Role of the Chief Academic*

Officer, eds. J. Martin, J. E. Samels, and Associates, 81–103. Baltimore, Md.: The Johns Hopkins University Press.

Hearn, J. C., and M. K. McLendon. 2005. "Sunshine Laws in Higher Education." *Academe* 91 (3): 28–31.

Hebel, S. 2004. State regents: Should they be elected or appointed? [Electronic version]. *The Chronicle of Higher Education* (October 15).

Heenan, D. A., and W. Bennis. 1999. *"Co-Leaders: The Power of Great Partnerships."* New York: John Wiley & Sons.

Hermalin, B. E. 2004. "Higher Education Boards of Trustees." In *Governing Academia*, ed. R. G. Ehrenberg, 28–48. Ithaca, N.Y.: Cornell University Press.

Hines, E. R. 2000. "The Governance of Higher Education." In *Higher Education: Handbook of Theory and Research*. Vol. 15, ed. J. C. Smart, 105–55. New York: Agathon Press.

Hoover, E. 2006. Study of predictors of success in college finds students taking increasingly complex paths to degrees [Electronic version]. *The Chronicle of Higher Education* (February 15).

Hurd, R., and J. Bloom, with B. H. Johnson. 1998. *Directory of Faculty Contracts and Bargaining Agents in Institutions of Higher Education*. Vol. 24. New York: National Center for the Study of Collective Bargaining in Higher Education and the Professions, School of Public Affairs, Baruch College, The City University of New York.

Ikenberry, S. O. 1999. "Past Triumphs, Future Challenges: A Conversation with Clark Kerr." *The Presidency* (Winter): 12–19.

Ingram, R. T. 1997. *Trustee Responsibilities: A Guide for Governing Boards of Public Institutions*. Washington, D.C.: Association of Governing Boards of Universities and Colleges.

Jacobson, J. 2006. Temple U. revises its procedures in aftermath of 'academic bill of rights' hearings [Electronic version]. *The Chronicle of Higher Education* (July 21).

Jones, D. P., P. T. Ewell, and A. McGuinness. 1998. *The Challenges and Opportunities Facing Higher Education: An Agenda for Policy Research*. San Jose, Calif.: The National Center for Policy in Higher Education.

Julius, D. J., V. Baldridge, and J. Pfeffer. 1999. "A Memo from Machiavelli." *The Journal of Higher Education* 70 (2): 113–33.

Julius, D. J., and P. J. Gumport. 2002. "Graduate Student Unionization: Catalysts and Consequences." *The Review of Higher Education* 26 (2): 187–216.

Kaplan, G. E. 2004. "How Academic Ships Actually Navigate." In *Governing Academia*, ed. R. G. Ehrenberg, 165–208. Ithaca, N.Y.: Cornell University Press.

Katz, R. N. 1999. "Competitive Strategies for Higher Education in the Information Age." In *Dancing with the Devil: Information Technology and the New Competition in Higher Education*, eds. R. N. Katz and Associates, 27–49. San Francisco: Jossey-Bass.

Keller, G. 1983. *Academic Strategy: The Management Revolution in American Higher Education*. Baltimore, Md.: The Johns Hopkins University Press.

———. 2001. "The New Demographics of Higher Education." *The Review of Higher Education* 24 (3): 219–35.

Kellogg Commission on the Future of State and Land-Grant Universities. 1996. *Taking Charge of Change: Renewing the Promise of State and Land-Grant Universities*. Washington, D.C.: National Association of State Universities and Land-Grant Colleges.

———. 1999. *Returning to Our Roots: The Engaged Institution*. Washington, D.C.: National Association of State Universities and Land-Grant Colleges.

Kerr, C. 1963. *The Uses of the University*. Cambridge, Mass.: Harvard University Press.

Kerr, C., and M. L. Gade 1989. *The Guardians: Boards of Trustees of American Colleges and Universities*. Washington, D.C.: Association of Governing Boards of Universities and Colleges.

Kezar, A. 2004. "What Is More Important to Effective Governance: Relationships, Trust, and Leadership, or Structures and Formal Processes?" In *Restructuring Shared Governance in Higher Education*, eds. W. G. Tierney and V. M. Lechuga, 35–46. New Directions for Higher Education no. 127. San Francisco: Jossey-Bass.

Kezar, A., and P. Eckel. 2004. "Meeting Today's Governance Challenges: A Synthesis of the Literature and Examination of a Future Agenda for Scholarship." *Journal of Higher Education* 75 (4): 371–99.

Kezar, A., W. Tierney, and J. Minor. 2004a. *Assessing Public Board Performance*. Los Angeles: Center for Higher Education Public Policy Analysis.

———. 2004b. *Selection and Appointment of Trustees to Public College and University Boards*. Los Angeles: Center for Higher Education Public Policy Analysis.

Kirp, D. L. 2003. *Shakespeare, Einstein, and the Bottom Line: The Marketing of Higher Education*. Cambridge, Mass.: Harvard University Press.

———. 2005. "This Little Student Went to Market." In *Declining by Degrees: Higher Education at Risk*, eds. R. H. Hersh and J. Merrow, 113–29. New York: Palgrave Macmillan.

Knight Higher Education Collaborative. 2002. "Of Precept, Policy, and Practice." *Policy Perspectives* 11 (1): 1–10.

Kotler, P., and P. E. Murphy. 1981. "Strategic Planning for Higher Education." *Journal of Higher Education* 52 (5): 470–89.

Leatherman, C. 2000. Union movement at private colleges awakens after a 20-year slumber [Electronic version]. *The Chronicle of Higher Education* (January 21).

Lederman, D. 2006. The hurdles ahead [Electronic version]. *Inside Higher Education* (May 22).

Levine, A. 2000. Higher education in the digital age [Electronic version]. Excerpt from an essay [same title] by A. Levine in the 1998 Teachers College Annual Report, Columbia University. *Student Affairs On-Line* 1 (1).

Longanecker, D. C. 2006. "Governing for Real." In *Governance and the Public Good*, ed. W. G. Tierney, 95–115. Albany, N.Y.: State University of New York Press.

Maitland, C., and G. Rhoades. 2001. "Unions and Faculty Governance." In *The National Education Association 2001 Almanac of Higher Education*, 27–33. Washington, D.C.: National Education Association.

Martin, J., J. E. Samels, and Associates. 1997. *First among Equals: The Role of the Chief Academic Officer*. Baltimore, Md.: The Johns Hopkins University Press.

Massachusetts Board of Higher Education and Public Education Nominating Council. N.d. *Trusteeship at Massachusetts Public Colleges and Universities: An Introduction to Serving on a Public Higher Education Board of Trustees*. Boston: Massachusetts Board of Higher Education and Public Education Nominating Council.

Massy, W. F. 2003. *Honoring the Trust: Quality and Cost Containment in Higher Education*. Bolton, Mass.: Anker Publishing.

Mathews, J. 2005. "Caveat Lector: Unexamined Assumptions about Quality in Higher Education." In *Declining by Degrees: Higher Education at Risk*, eds. R. H. Hersh and J. Merrow, 47–59. New York: Palgrave Macmillan.

McGuinness, A. C., Jr. 2002. *Reflections on Postsecondary Governance Changes*. ECS Policy Brief. Denver: Education Commission of the States.

———. 2003. *State Policy Leadership in the Public Interest: Is Anyone at Home?* Background paper prepared for the Macalester Forum on Higher Education, June, at Macalester College, Saint Paul, Minn. Boulder, Colo: National Center for Higher Education Management Systems.

McPherson, M. S., and M. O. Schapiro. 1998. *The Student Aid Game: Meeting Need and Rewarding Talent in American Higher Education*. Princeton, N.J.: Princeton University Press.

Meacham, J., and J. G. Gaff. 2006. Learning goals in mission statements: Implications for educational leadership [Electronic version]. *Liberal Education* (Winter).

Miller, M. T., and J. Caplow, eds. 2003. *Policy and University Faculty Governance*. Greenwich, Conn.: Information Age Publishing.

Minor, J. T. 2003. "Assessing the Senate." *American Behavioral Scientist* 46 (7): 960–77.

———. 2004. "Understanding Faculty Senates: Moving from Mystery to Models." *The Review of Higher Education* 27 (3): 343–63.

Moore, J. W. 2003. "Planning, Politics, and Presidential Leadership." In *Connecting the Dots … The Essence of Planning: The Best of Planning for Higher Education 1997–2003*, ed. Rod Rose, 13–19. Ann Arbor, Mich.: Society for College and University Planning.

Morrill, R. L. 2002. *Strategic Leadership in Academic Affairs: Clarifying the Board's Responsibilities*. Washington, D.C.: Association of Governing Boards of Universities and Colleges.

———. 2003. *The Board's Responsibilities for Academic Affairs*. Washington, D.C.: Association of Governing Boards of Universities and Colleges.

Mortenson, T. G. 2001. College enrollment by age: 1950 to 2000 [Electronic version]. *Postsecondary Education OPPORTUNITY*, no. 113.

———. 2003. College continuation rates for recent high school graduates, 1959–2002 [Electronic version]. *Postsecondary Education OPPORTUNITY*, no. 132.

Mortimer, K. P., and T. R. McConnell. 1978. *Sharing Authority Effectively*. San Francisco: Jossey-Bass.

Mortimer, K. P., and C. O. Sathre. 2006. "Be Mission Centered, Market Smart, and Politically Savvy: The Art of Governance." In *Governance and the Public Good*, ed. W. G. Tierney, 73–93. Albany, N.Y.: State University of New York Press.

Nason, J. W. 1982. *The Nature of Trusteeship: The Role and Responsibilities of College and University Boards*. Washington, D.C.: Association of Governing Boards of Universities and Colleges.

National Center for Public Policy and Higher Education. 1998. A very public agenda: A national roundtable examines the role of public policy in shaping higher education [Electronic version]. *National Crosstalk* 6 (3).

Newman, F. 1987. *Choosing Quality: Reducing Conflict between the State and the University*. Denver: Education Commission of the States.

Newman, F., and L. Couturier. 2001. *The New Competitive Arena: Market Forces Invade the Academy*. Providence, R.I.: The Futures Project.

Newman, F., L. Couturier, and J. Scurry. 2004. *The Future of Higher Education: Rhetoric, Reality, and the Risks of the Market*. San Francisco: Jossey-Bass.

Paradise, L. V. 2004. The perils of provosting [Electronic version]. *The Chronicle of Higher Education* (January 16).

Pew Higher Education Roundtable. 1993. "A Transatlantic Dialogue." *Policy Perspectives* 5 (1): 1–11.

Pfeffer, J. 1992. *Managing with Power: Politics and Influence in Organizations*. Boston: Harvard Business School Press.

Pusser, B., and I. Ordorika. 2001. "Bringing Political Theory to University Governance: A Comparative Analysis of Governing Boards at the University of California and the Universidad Nacional Autonoma de Mexico." In *Higher Education: Handbook of Theory and Research*. Vol. 16, ed. J. C. Smart, 147–94. New York: Agathon Press.

Pusser, B., and S. E. Turner. 2004. "Nonprofit and For-Profit Governance in Higher Education." In *Governing Academia*, ed. R. G. Ehrenberg, 235–57. Ithaca, N.Y.: Cornell University Press.

Ramo, K. 1998. *Assessing the Faculty's Role in Shared Governance*. Washington, D.C.: American Association of University Professors.

Rhoades, G. 1998. *Managed Professionals: Unionized Faculty and the Restructuring of Academic Labor*. Albany, N.Y.: State University of New York Press.

———. 2005. Capitalism, academic style, and shared governance [Electronic version]. *Academe* 91 (3).

Rhoades, G., and R. A. Rhoads. 2002. "The Public Discourse of U.S. Graduate Employee Unions: Social Movement Identities, Ideologies, and Strategies." *The Review of Higher Education* 26 (2): 163–86.

Richardson, J. T. 1999. "Centralizing Governance Isn't Simply Wrong: It's Bad Business, Too." *The Chronicle of Higher Education* (February 12): B9.

Rittel, H. W. J., and M. M. Webber. 1973. "Dilemmas in a General Theory of Planning." *Policy Sciences* 4:155–69.

Rosser, V. J. 2002. "Governance." In *Higher Education in the United States: An Encyclopedia*, eds. J. Forest and K. Kinser, 279–84. Santa Barbara, Calif.: ABC-CLIO Publishers.

Rowley, D. J., and H. Sherman. 2003. "Implementing the Strategic Plan." In *Connecting the Dots ... the Essence of Planning: The Best of Planning for Higher Education 1997–2003*, ed. Rod Rose, 241–50. Ann Arbor, Mich.: Society for College and University Planning.

Schmidtlein, F. A., and T. H. Milton. 1988–89. "College and University Planning: Perspectives from a Nation-Wide Study." *Planning for Higher Education* 17 (3): 1–19.

Schuster, J., D. G. Smith, K. A. Corak, and M. M. Yamada. 1994. *Strategic Governance: How to Make Big Decisions Better*. Washington, D.C.: Oryx Press.

Seymour, D. 1995. *Once Upon a Campus: Lessons for Improving Quality and Productivity in Higher Education*. Westport, Conn.: American Council on Education and Oryx Press.

Shirley, R. C. 1988. "Strategic Planning: An Overview." *New Directions for Higher Education* 16 (4): 5–14.

Shulock, N., and M. E. Harrison. 2003. "Integrating Planning, Assessment, and Resource Allocation." In *Connecting the Dots ... the Essence of Planning: The Best of Planning for Higher Education 1997–2003*, ed. Rod Rose, 137–43. Ann Arbor, Mich.: Society for College and University Planning.

Slaughter, S., and L. L. Leslie. 1997. *Academic Capitalism*. Baltimore, Md.: The Johns Hopkins University Press.

Smallwood, S. 2004. "Union Blues in the Sunshine State." *The Chronicle of Higher Education* (April 2): A10-A12.

Swenk, J. 1999. "Planning Failures: Decision Cultural Clashes." *The Review of Higher Education* 23 (1): 1–21.

Tierney, W. G. 2001. "Why Committees Don't Work: Creating a Structure for Change." *Academe* 87 (3): 25–29.

———, ed. 2004. *Competing Conceptions of Academic Governance: Negotiating the Perfect Storm*. Baltimore, Md.: The Johns Hopkins University Press.

————. 2005. When divorce is not an option: The board and the faculty [Electronic version]. *Academe* 91 (3).

————, ed. 2006. *Governance and the Public Good*. Albany, N.Y.: State University of New York Press.

Tierney, W. G., and K. Holley. 2005. Shared governance under fire: Reform and renewal [Electronic version]. *Academe* 91 (3).

Tierney, W. G., and V. M. Lechuga, eds. 2004. *Restructuring Shared Governance in Higher Education*. New Directions for Higher Education no. 127. San Francisco: Jossey-Bass.

Trow, M. 1996. "Trust, Markets and Accountability in Higher Education: A Comparative Perspective." *Higher Education Policy* 9 (4): 309–24.

U.S. Department of Education. National Center for Education Statistics. 2001. *Institutional Policies and Practices: Results from the 1999 National Study of Postsecondary Faculty, Institution Survey*. NCES 2001–201. Washington, D.C.: U.S. Department of Education.

————. 2003. *Digest of Education Statistics, 2002*. NCES 2003–060. Washington, D.C.: U.S. Department of Education.

————. 2004. *The Condition of Education 2004*. NCES 2004–077. Washington, D.C.: U.S. Department of Education.

University of Hawai'i. Institutional Research Office. 2004. Undergraduate students with other college experience. Unpublished report and analysis prepared for author.

Wellman, J. V. 2006. "Rethinking State Governance for Higher Education." In *Governance and the Public Good*, ed. W. G. Tierney, 51–72. Albany, N.Y.: State University of New York Press.

Zemsky, R., and W. F. Massy. 1995. "Toward an Understanding of Our Current Predicaments." *Change* (November/December): 41–49.

Zemsky, R., G. R. Wegner, and W. F. Massy. 2005. *Remaking the American University: Market-Smart and Mission-Centered*. New Brunswick, N.J.: Rutgers University Press.

INDEX

About the Authors

KENNETH P. MORTIMER is President Emeritus of Western Washington University and President and Chancellor Emeritus of the University of Hawai'i. Since 2002, he has been a Senior Associate at The National Center for Higher Education Management Systems. He has been Director of the Center for the Study of Higher Education and a Vice President and Vice Provost at Pennsylvania State University. He holds an A.B. from the University of Pennsylvania, an M.B.A. from the Wharton School, and a Ph.D. from the University of California, Berkeley. Currently he is engaged in writing, consulting, and serving on boards. He resides in Bellingham, Washington.

COLLEEN O'BRIEN SATHRE is Vice President Emeritus, Planning and Policy, of the University of Hawai'i, where she served the university system as the chief academic planning officer for more than 25 years. She managed efforts that produced university mission statements and strategic plans, tuition schedules, university centers on neighbor islands, performance indicators, a reorganization of university information technology services, and numerous board and executive policies. She holds a B.A. from the College of St. Benedict, St. Joseph, MN, and an M.A. and Ph.D. from the University of Minnesota. She is currently engaged in writing and consulting and resides in Honolulu, Hawai'i.